The Australian Women's Weekly
cookbooks

Getting home after a long day at work, the last thing I want to do is spend hours trying to get dinner on the table. This book is the answer to all my prayers – and probably yours, too. *Midweek Meals in Minutes* is filled with appealing, wholesome main-meal ideas (plus a chapter on desserts) that can be ready to eat in around half an hour. No matter what your family is in the mood for – a stir-fry, main-course salad or pasta dish – you'll be able to satisfy their appetites when you turn the pages of this book.

Pamela Clark

Food Director

contents

stir-fried chicken and gai larn

PREPARATION TIME **10 MINUTES** COOKING TIME **15 MINUTES**

Gai larn, also known as gai lum or chinese broccoli, can be found
in Asian food stores and many greengrocers.

2 tablespoons sesame oil
500g chicken thigh fillets, sliced thinly
2 teaspoons sambal oelek
190g can sliced water chestnuts, drained
227g can bamboo shoot strips, drained
1 large red capsicum (350g), sliced thinly
⅓ cup (80ml) kecap manis
500g gai larn, chopped coarsely
2 cups (160g) bean sprouts

1 Heat half of the oil in wok or large frying pan; stir-fry chicken,
   in batches, until browned lightly.
2 Heat remaining oil in same wok; stir-fry sambal, water chestnuts,
   bamboo shoots and capsicum for 2 minutes.
3 Return chicken to wok with kecap manis and gai larn; stir-fry until
   gai larn is just wilted and chicken is cooked through. Remove from heat;
   stir in sprouts.

SERVES 4
per serving 18.7g fat; 1347kJ (322 cal)

chicken and leek puff pastry squares

PREPARATION TIME **20 MINUTES (PLUS COOLING TIME)** COOKING TIME **25 MINUTES**

40g butter
1 small leek (200g), sliced thinly
2 cloves garlic, crushed
450g chicken breast fillets, chopped coarsely
2 tablespoons cornflour
½ cup (125ml) dry white wine
½ cup (125ml) chicken stock
½ cup (125ml) cream
2 sheets ready-rolled puff pastry
1 egg, beaten lightly

1 Preheat oven to moderately hot.
2 Melt butter in large frying pan; cook leek and garlic, stirring, until leek softens. Add chicken; cook, stirring, until chicken is browned lightly.
3 Add blended cornflour and wine, then stock and cream; stir until mixture boils and thickens. Reduce heat; simmer, uncovered, 5 minutes. Spread onto tray; cool 10 minutes.
4 Cut each sheet of pastry in half; place pastry pieces on oiled oven trays. Spoon a quarter of the chicken mixture onto half of one piece, leaving 1cm border; brush edges with egg. Fold pastry over to enclose filling; pinch edges together to seal. Cut two slits in top of pastry square; brush with egg. Repeat with remaining pastry, chicken mixture and egg. Bake, uncovered, in moderately hot oven about 15 minutes or until just browned.

SERVES 4
per serving 33.9g fat; 2076kJ (496 cal)

TIP Uncooked parcels can be frozen, covered tightly, for up to a month. Thaw overnight in the refrigerator before baking.

greek salad with smoked chicken

PREPARATION TIME **20 MINUTES**

Smoked chicken breast may be slightly pink, like bacon and ham, but this does not mean it is undercooked.

1 small red onion (100g),
   sliced thinly
200g fetta cheese, crumbled
250g grape tomatoes
400g smoked chicken breast,
   sliced thinly
200g baby spinach leaves
⅔ cup (110g) seeded
   kalamata olives
1 medium red capsicum (200g),
   sliced thinly
⅓ cup (80ml) olive oil
¼ cup (60ml) lemon juice
1 clove garlic, crushed

1 Combine onion, cheese,
tomatoes, chicken, spinach,
olives and capsicum in
large bowl.
2 Combine remaining ingredients
in screw-top jar; shake well.
Drizzle dressing over salad;
toss gently to combine.

SERVES 4
per serving 38.3g fat;
2252kJ (538 cal)

TIP A large barbecued chicken
can be used instead of the
smoked chicken; discard bones
and skin, then chop the meat
coarsely before tossing with
remaining salad ingredients.

teriyaki chicken and cashew stir-fry with noodles

PREPARATION TIME **20 MINUTES** COOKING TIME **15 MINUTES**

450g hokkien noodles
2 tablespoons peanut oil
1kg chicken thigh fillets,
    sliced thinly
1 medium brown onion (150g),
    sliced thinly
1 clove garlic, crushed
2 teaspoons grated fresh ginger
1 medium red capsicum (200g),
    sliced thinly
1 tablespoon brown sugar
2 tablespoons soy sauce
½ cup (125ml) teriyaki sauce
500g choy sum,
    chopped coarsely
½ cup (75g) unsalted
    roasted cashews

1 Place noodles in medium
  heatproof bowl; cover with
  boiling water, separate with
  fork, drain.
2 Heat half of the oil in wok or
  large frying pan; stir-fry chicken,
  in batches, until browned lightly.
3 Heat remaining oil in same wok;
  stir-fry onion, garlic, ginger and
  capsicum about 3 minutes or
  until onion is just tender.
4 Return chicken to wok with
  sugar, sauces and choy sum;
  stir-fry until chicken is cooked
  through and choy sum wilted.
  Add noodles and half of the
  nuts; toss gently until heated
  through. Serve stir-fry topped
  with remaining nuts.

SERVES 6
per serving 25.7g fat;
2128kJ (508 cal)

9

moroccan chicken with couscous

PREPARATION TIME **10 MINUTES (PLUS STANDING TIME)** COOKING TIME **10 MINUTES**

Preserved lemons – salted lemons preserved in a mixture of olive oil and lemon juice – are a North African specialty, usually added to casseroles and tagines to impart a salty-sour acidic flavour. They're available from good food shops and delicatessens. Rinse preserved lemons well under cold water, discard flesh then finely chop the rind. Moroccan marinade is a bottled blend of garlic, capsicum, chilli, lemon and various spices, and can be found at your local supermarket.

4 single chicken breast fillets (680g)
⅓ cup (80ml) moroccan marinade
2 cups (500ml) vegetable stock
2 cups (400g) couscous
20g butter
1 small red onion (100g), sliced thinly
2 fresh small red thai chillies, seeded, chopped finely
½ cup (110g) coarsely chopped seeded prunes
⅓ cup (45g) slivered almonds, toasted
½ cup coarsely chopped fresh mint
¼ cup (45g) finely chopped preserved lemon

1 Toss chicken in large bowl with marinade; stand 10 minutes. Cook chicken, in batches, on heated oiled grill plate (or grill or barbecue) until browned lightly and cooked through. Stand 5 minutes; slice chicken thickly.
2 Meanwhile, bring stock to a boil in medium saucepan. Remove from heat; stir in couscous and butter. Cover; stand 5 minutes or until liquid is absorbed, fluffing couscous with fork occasionally. Stir in remaining ingredients. Serve chicken on couscous.

SERVES 4
per serving 16.2g fat; 3117kJ (745 cal)

oven-baked risotto with chicken, rocket and semi-dried tomato

PREPARATION TIME **10 MINUTES** COOKING TIME **35 MINUTES**

1 tablespoon olive oil
1 large brown onion (200g), sliced thinly
2 cloves garlic, crushed
2 cups (400g) arborio rice
¾ cup (180ml) dry white wine
1 litre (4 cups) chicken stock
4 single chicken breast fillets (680g)
100g baby rocket leaves
100g semi-dried tomatoes, sliced thinly
½ cup (40g) finely grated parmesan cheese
1 tablespoon coarsely chopped fresh flat-leaf parsley

1 Preheat oven to moderate.
2 Heat oil in shallow 3-litre (12 cup) flameproof baking dish; cook onion and garlic, stirring, until onion softens. Add rice; stir to coat in onion mixture. Stir in wine and stock; bring to a boil. Place chicken, in single layer, on top of rice mixture. Transfer dish to moderate oven; bake, covered, about 25 minutes or until rice is tender and chicken is cooked through. Remove chicken; stand chicken 5 minutes. Slice thickly.
3 Stir rocket, tomato and a third of the cheese into risotto; serve risotto topped with chicken. Sprinkle remaining cheese and parsley over chicken.

SERVES 4
per serving 21.3g fat; 3414kJ (815 cal)

baked bocconcini and pesto chicken with garlicky potatoes

PREPARATION TIME **15 MINUTES** COOKING TIME **30 MINUTES**

4 large potatoes (800g)
4 cloves garlic, peeled
1 tablespoon olive oil
4 single chicken breast
　fillets (680g)
2 tablespoons bottled
　basil pesto
100g drained char-grilled
　capsicum in oil
150g bocconcini cheese,
　sliced thinly

1 Preheat oven to moderately hot.
2 Cut unpeeled potatoes into
　5mm slices; toss with garlic and
　oil in large baking dish. Roast,
　uncovered, in moderately
　hot oven 10 minutes,
　stirring occasionally.
3 Meanwhile, using sharp knife,
　score each fillet, taking care
　not to cut all the way through.
　Spread fillets with pesto; top
　with capsicum and cheese.
　Place fillets, topping-side up,
　on oiled wire rack; sit rack over
　potato in baking dish. Bake,
　uncovered, about 20 minutes or
　until chicken is cooked through.
　Serve chicken with potatoes.

SERVES 4
per serving 24.8g fat;
2421kJ (578 cal)

honey soy chicken salad

PREPARATION TIME **20 MINUTES** COOKING TIME **15 MINUTES**

You need about a quarter of a small savoy cabbage for this recipe.

600g chicken breast fillets, sliced thinly
2 tablespoons soy sauce
⅓ cup (115g) honey
1 clove garlic, crushed
4 fresh small red thai chillies, seeded, chopped finely
300g snow peas
1 small carrot (120g)
1 tablespoon peanut oil
2 cups (160g) finely shredded savoy cabbage
1 medium yellow capsicum (200g), sliced thinly
1 medium red capsicum (200g), sliced thinly
1 lebanese cucumber (130g), seeded, sliced thinly
4 green onions, sliced thinly
½ cup loosely packed fresh mint leaves
2 tablespoons lime juice
2 teaspoons sesame oil

1 Place chicken in medium bowl with sauce, honey, garlic and half of the
   chilli; toss to coat chicken in chilli mixture. Cover; refrigerate until required.
2 Boil, steam or microwave snow peas until just tender; drain.
   Rinse immediately under cold water; drain. Using vegetable peeler,
   slice carrot into ribbons.
3 Heat peanut oil in wok or large frying pan; stir-fry drained chicken,
   in batches, until browned and cooked through.
4 Place chicken, snow peas and carrot in large serving bowl with
   remaining ingredients and remaining chilli; toss gently to combine.

SERVES 4
per serving 15.8g fat; 1778kJ (425 cal)

TIP You can use a large barbecued chicken instead of the breast fillets,
if you prefer; discard bones and skin, then shred meat coarsely before
tossing with remaining salad ingredients.

thai chicken and lychee salad

PREPARATION TIME 20 MINUTES

You need to buy a large barbecued chicken weighing about 1kg for this recipe; discard skin and bones, then shred the meat coarsely.

3 cups (480g) shredded
   cooked chicken
565g can lychees in syrup,
   drained, halved
1 small red onion (100g),
   sliced thinly
8 green onions, sliced thinly
2 cups (160g) bean sprouts
½ cup firmly packed fresh
   mint leaves
½ cup firmly packed fresh
   coriander leaves
1 teaspoon finely grated
   lime rind
1 teaspoon sambal oelek
¼ cup (60ml) lime juice
1 teaspoon sesame oil
1 tablespoon brown sugar
2 teaspoons fish sauce

1 Combine chicken, lychees, onions, sprouts, mint and coriander in large bowl.
2 Combine remaining ingredients in screw-top jar; shake well. Drizzle dressing over salad; toss gently to combine.

SERVES 4
per serving 10.5g fat;
1265kJ (302 cal)

lemony chicken with baby spinach salad

PREPARATION TIME **15 MINUTES**   COOKING TIME **15 MINUTES**

12 chicken tenderloins (900g)
2 tablespoons lemon juice
1 tablespoon fresh thyme leaves
½ cup (125ml) olive oil
100g baby spinach leaves
1 small red onion (100g),
   chopped finely
250g cherry tomatoes, halved
80g snow pea sprouts
⅓ cup (80ml) red wine vinegar
½ teaspoon dijon mustard

1 Place chicken in large bowl with
juice, thyme and 2 tablespoons
of the oil; toss to coat chicken in
lemon mixture. Cook chicken,
in batches, on heated oiled grill
plate (or grill or barbecue) until
browned and cooked through.
2 Meanwhile, combine spinach,
onion, tomato and sprouts in
large bowl. Combine remaining
oil, vinegar and mustard in
screw-top jar; shake well.
Drizzle dressing over salad;
toss gently to combine. Serve
salad topped with chicken.

SERVES 4
per serving 41.9g fat;
2581kJ (616 cal)

chicken jambalaya

PREPARATION TIME **15 MINUTES** COOKING TIME **30 MINUTES**

One of the most well-known American creole dishes, jambalaya is believed to have been devised when a New Orleans cook named Jean tossed together – or "balayez" in the dialect of Louisiana – various leftovers and came up with such a delicious dish that diners named it "Jean Balayez". We used a commercially packaged basmati and wild rice blend in this recipe, but you can use all basmati rice if you prefer.

1 tablespoon olive oil
1 medium brown onion (150g), chopped coarsely
1 medium red capsicum (200g), chopped coarsely
1 clove garlic, crushed
2 trimmed celery sticks (150g), sliced thinly
2 fresh small red thai chillies, seeded, sliced thinly
1½ cups (300g) basmati and wild rice blend
½ cup (125ml) dry white wine
2½ cups (625ml) chicken stock
425g can crushed tomatoes
1 tablespoon tomato paste
700g chicken and herb sausages
⅓ cup coarsely chopped fresh coriander

1 Heat oil in large saucepan; cook onion, capsicum, garlic, celery and chilli, stirring, until vegetables soften. Stir in rice, wine, stock, undrained tomatoes and paste; bring to a boil. Reduce heat; simmer, covered, about 20 minutes or until liquid is absorbed.
2 Meanwhile, cook sausages, uncovered, in large frying pan until browned and cooked through. Drain on absorbent paper; slice thickly.
3 Stir sausage and coriander into jambalaya mixture just before serving.

SERVES 4
per serving 45.7g fat; 3506kJ (838 cal)

chicken, zucchini and corn soup

PREPARATION TIME **15 MINUTES**   COOKING TIME **10 MINUTES**

You need to buy a large barbecued chicken, weighing about 1kg, for this recipe; discard skin and bones, chop the meat coarsely.

20g butter
1 large brown onion (200g), chopped finely
1 clove garlic, crushed
2 medium zucchini (240g), grated coarsely
1 litre (4 cups) chicken stock
420g can creamed corn
3 cups (480g) coarsely chopped cooked chicken
½ cup (125ml) cream

1 Melt butter in large saucepan; cook onion and garlic, stirring, until onion softens. Add zucchini; cook, stirring, 1 minute. Add stock; bring to a boil.
2 Stir in corn and chicken, reduce heat; simmer, uncovered, until chicken is hot. Stir in cream just before serving.

SERVES 4
per serving 28.6g fat; 2066kJ (494 cal)

chicken tikka drumettes

PREPARATION TIME **10 MINUTES** COOKING TIME **25 MINUTES**

12 chicken drumettes (960g)
⅓ cup (100g) tikka masala paste
½ cup (140g) yogurt
2 cups (400g) jasmine rice
12 small pappadums
¼ cup coarsely chopped
   fresh coriander
⅓ cup (110g) mild lime pickle

1 Preheat oven to moderately hot.
2 Place chicken in large bowl
   with combined paste and
   2 tablespoons of the yogurt;
   toss to coat chicken in paste
   mixture. Place chicken, in single
   layer, on wire rack in large
   baking dish. Roast, uncovered,
   in moderately hot oven about
   20 minutes or until chicken is
   browned and cooked through.
3 Meanwhile, cook rice in large
   saucepan of boiling water,
   uncovered, until just tender;
   drain. Cover to keep warm.
4 Place 3 pappadums around edge
   of microwave oven turntable.
   Cook on HIGH (100%) about
   30 seconds or until puffed. Repeat
   with remaining pappadums.
5 Combine coriander and
   remaining yogurt in small bowl.
   Serve chicken on rice drizzled
   with yogurt mixture; accompany
   with lime pickle and pappadums.

SERVES 4
per serving 21.7g fat;
3515kJ (840 cal)

TIP Pappadums can also be
deep-fried in vegetable oil.

prawn tamarind stir-fry with bok choy

PREPARATION TIME **25 MINUTES** COOKING TIME **10 MINUTES**

1kg uncooked medium king prawns
2 tablespoons peanut oil
4 green onions, sliced thinly lengthways
4 cloves garlic, sliced thinly
1 teaspoon cornflour
½ cup (125ml) vegetable stock
2 tablespoons oyster sauce
1 tablespoon tamarind puree
1 teaspoon sambal oelek
2 teaspoons sesame oil
1 tablespoon lime juice
1 tablespoon brown sugar
350g yellow patty-pan squash, sliced thickly
300g sugar snap peas, trimmed
800g baby bok choy, chopped coarsely

1 Shell and devein prawns, leaving tails intact.
2 Heat half of the peanut oil in wok or large frying pan; stir-fry onion and garlic, separately, until browned lightly. Drain on absorbent paper.
3 Blend cornflour and stock in small jug; stir in sauce, tamarind, sambal, sesame oil, juice and sugar.
4 Heat remaining peanut oil in same wok; stir-fry prawns, in batches, until changed in colour and almost cooked through. Stir-fry squash in same wok until just tender. Add cornflour mixture; stir-fry until sauce boils and thickens slightly. Return prawns to wok with peas and bok choy; stir-fry until bok choy just wilts and prawns are cooked through. Serve stir-fry with steamed jasmine rice and topped with reserved onion and garlic.

SERVES 4
per serving 13.3g fat; 1329kJ (317 cal)

salt and lemon-pepper squid with lemon mayonnaise

PREPARATION TIME **15 MINUTES**   COOKING TIME **15 MINUTES**

600g squid hoods
½ cup (70g) plain flour
2 teaspoons coarse cooking salt
1 tablespoon lemon pepper
vegetable oil, for deep-frying
120g mesclun

LEMON MAYONNAISE
1 cup (300g) mayonnaise
¼ cup (60ml) lemon juice
1 tablespoon boiling water

1 Halve squid hoods lengthways, score the insides in crosshatch pattern then cut each half lengthways into five pieces. Toss squid in medium bowl with combined flour, salt and pepper until coated; shake off excess.
2 Make lemon mayonnaise.
3 Heat oil in wok or large saucepan; deep-fry squid, in batches, until tender and browned lightly. Drain on absorbent paper.
4 Place mesclun with a quarter of the lemon mayonnaise in medium bowl; toss gently to combine. Serve squid and mesclun salad with remaining lemon mayonnaise.
LEMON MAYONNAISE Whisk ingredients in small bowl until well combined.

SERVES 4
per serving 66.8g fat;
3270kJ (781 cal)

TIP We used whole-egg mayonnaise in this recipe.

tuna, olive and rocket pasta

PREPARATION TIME **15 MINUTES**   COOKING TIME **15 MINUTES**

2 tablespoons olive oil
1 tablespoon finely grated
  lemon rind
¼ cup (60ml) lemon juice
1 clove garlic, crushed
1 tablespoon dijon mustard
250g angel hair pasta
425g can yellowfin tuna chunks
  in olive oil, drained, flaked
⅓ cup (55g) seeded kalamata
  olives, quartered lengthways
250g cherry tomatoes, halved
⅓ cup (50g) toasted pine nuts
100g baby rocket leaves

1 Combine oil, rind, juice, garlic
and mustard in screw-top jar;
shake well.
2 Cook pasta in large saucepan
of boiling water, uncovered,
until just tender.
3 Meanwhile, combine remaining
ingredients in large bowl; add
drained pasta. Shake dressing
again before drizzling over pasta
mixture; toss gently to combine.

SERVES 4
per serving 29.9g fat;
2468kJ (590 cal)

TIP Angel hair pasta, also known
as capelli d'angelo, is a thin,
narrow pasta that cooks very
quickly. Do not overcook or
it will become starchy and
stodgy. This recipe is best
made just before serving.

sweet and sour fish on asian greens

PREPARATION TIME **20 MINUTES** COOKING TIME **20 MINUTES**

We used warehou fillets in this recipe; however, any moist, firm, white fish fillet can be used.

2 tablespoons peanut oil
1 large brown onion (200g), sliced thickly
2 teaspoons grated fresh ginger
1 medium red capsicum (200g), chopped coarsely
2 teaspoons cornflour
⅓ cup (80ml) water
½ cup (125ml) vegetable stock
⅓ cup (80ml) tomato sauce
2 tablespoons soy sauce
1 tablespoon malt vinegar
2 tablespoons lemon juice
4 x 200g firm white fish fillets
450g can pineapple pieces in syrup, drained
250g gai larn, chopped coarsely
200g baby bok choy, quartered
300g choy sum, chopped coarsely

1 Heat half of the oil in medium saucepan; cook onion, ginger
and capsicum, stirring, until capsicum is just tender. Add blended
cornflour and water with stock, sauces, vinegar and juice; cook,
stirring, until sauce boils and thickens slightly. Remove from heat.
2 Heat remaining oil in wok or large frying pan; cook fish, in batches,
1 minute each side. Return fish to wok with sauce and pineapple;
cook, uncovered, until fish is cooked through.
3 Meanwhile, boil, steam or microwave gai larn, bok choy and choy sum,
separately, until just wilted; drain. Divide vegetables among serving
plates; top with fish and sauce.

SERVES 4
per serving 14.2g fat; 1661kJ (397 cal)

seared ocean trout with bok choy

PREPARATION TIME **10 MINUTES** COOKING TIME **15 MINUTES**

1 litre (4 cups) water
¼ cup (60ml) soy sauce
1 star anise
1 teaspoon sambal oelek
1 tablespoon honey
800g baby bok choy,
    halved lengthways
1 tablespoon sesame oil
4 x 240g ocean trout fillets

1 Combine the water, sauce,
star anise, sambal and honey
in medium saucepan; bring to
a boil. Cook bok choy in boiling
stock until just wilted. Remove
bok choy; cover to keep warm.
Strain stock into medium bowl;
discard solids. Return stock to
heat; boil, uncovered, while
cooking fish.

2 Heat oil in large frying pan;
sear fish over high heat until
cooked as desired. Serve fish
on bok choy; drizzle with stock.

SERVES 4
per serving 14.2g fat;
1517kJ (362 cal)

serving suggestion Serve fish
with steamed jasmine rice and
wedges of lime.

salmon with mango and pineapple salsa

PREPARATION TIME **10 MINUTES**   COOKING TIME **10 MINUTES**

4 x 200g salmon cutlets

**MANGO AND
PINEAPPLE SALSA**
2 small mangoes (600g),
   chopped coarsely
1 small pineapple (800g),
   chopped coarsely
2 tablespoons coarsely chopped
   fresh mint
2 tablespoons coarsely chopped
   fresh coriander
2 fresh small red thai chillies,
   seeded, sliced thinly
2 green onions, sliced thinly
2 tablespoons lime juice
1 tablespoon light olive oil

1 Make mango and
   pineapple salsa.
2 Cook fish, in batches, on
   heated oiled grill plate
   (or grill or barbecue) until
   browned both sides and
   cooked as desired. Serve
   fish with salsa.
   MANGO AND PINEAPPLE SALSA
   Place ingredients in medium
   bowl; toss gently to combine.

SERVES 4
per serving 19.1g fat;
1793kJ (428 cal)

salmon fillo triangles

PREPARATION TIME **15 MINUTES** COOKING TIME **15 MINUTES**

20g butter
3 green onions, sliced thinly
1 small red capsicum (150g), chopped finely
2 tablespoons plain flour
¼ cup (60ml) milk
½ cup (125ml) cream
1 tablespoon lemon juice
1 tablespoon drained baby capers, rinsed
30g baby spinach leaves
400g can red salmon, drained, flaked
4 sheets fillo pastry
50g butter, melted
150g mesclun
200g cherry tomatoes, halved

1 Melt butter in medium frying pan; cook onion and capsicum, stirring, until onion softens. Add flour; cook, stirring, until mixture bubbles. Gradually add combined milk and cream; stir until mixture boils and thickens. Remove from heat; stir in juice, capers, spinach and salmon.
2 Preheat oven to moderately hot.
3 Brush one sheet of the fillo with a little of the melted butter; fold in half lengthways. Place a quarter of the salmon mixture at bottom of one narrow edge of fillo, leaving a 1cm border. Fold opposite corner of fillo diagonally across filling to form a triangle; continue folding to end of fillo piece, retaining triangle shape. Place triangle on lightly oiled oven tray, seam-side down; repeat with remaining fillo and salmon mixture.
4 Brush triangles with remaining melted butter; bake, uncovered, in moderately hot oven about 10 minutes or until browned lightly and heated through. Serve salmon triangles with mesclun and tomato.

SERVES 4
per serving 30.8g fat; 1843kJ (440 cal)

mediterranean-style mussels with linguine

PREPARATION TIME **20 MINUTES** COOKING TIME **15 MINUTES**

1kg large black mussels
2 tablespoons olive oil
1 small brown onion (80g),
   sliced thinly
3 cloves garlic, crushed
2 fresh small red thai chillies,
   seeded, chopped finely
⅓ cup (80ml) dry white wine
2 tablespoons lemon juice
4 medium egg tomatoes (300g),
   chopped coarsely
375g linguine
½ cup coarsely chopped
   fresh basil

1 Scrub mussels; remove beards.
2 Heat oil in large saucepan;
   cook onion, garlic and chilli,
   stirring, until onion softens.
   Add mussels with wine, juice
   and tomato; bring to a boil.
   Reduce heat; simmer, covered,
   stirring occasionally, about
   5 minutes or until mussels
   open (discard any that do not).
3 Meanwhile, cook pasta in
   large saucepan of boiling water,
   uncovered, until just tender;
   drain. Stir pasta into mussel
   mixture. Remove from heat;
   stir in basil.

SERVES 4
per serving 11.6g fat;
2002kJ (478 cal)

TIP We used a pre-packaged
combination of plain, spinach-
and tomato-flavoured linguine,
but you can use any long,
narrow pasta you like.

char-grilled cuttlefish, rocket and parmesan salad

PREPARATION TIME **20 MINUTES** COOKING TIME **10 MINUTES**

1kg cuttlefish hoods
2 tablespoons olive oil
1 tablespoon finely grated
    lemon rind
⅓ cup (80ml) lemon juice
1 clove garlic, crushed
150g rocket
150g semi-dried tomatoes,
    drained, chopped coarsely
1 small red onion (100g),
    sliced thinly
1 tablespoon drained
    baby capers, rinsed
80g parmesan cheese, shaved
2 tablespoons balsamic vinegar
⅓ cup (80ml) olive oil, extra

1 Halve cuttlefish lengthways,
  score insides in crosshatch
  pattern then cut into 5cm strips.
  Combine cuttlefish in medium
  bowl with oil, rind, juice
  and garlic, cover; refrigerate
  10 minutes.
2 Meanwhile, combine rocket,
  tomato, onion, capers and
  cheese in large bowl.
3 Drain cuttlefish; discard
  marinade. Cook cuttlefish, in
  batches, on heated oiled grill
  plate (or grill or barbecue) until
  browned and cooked through.
4 Add cuttlefish to salad with
  combined vinegar and extra oil;
  toss gently to combine.

SERVES 4
per serving 41.3g fat;
2750kJ (657 cal)

risotto marinara

PREPARATION TIME **10 MINUTES** COOKING TIME **25 MINUTES**

This quick and easy version of the classic requires no pots or pans –
just one bowl and a microwave oven – so it's the perfect meal for
risotto lovers who have no time to waste.

60g butter
1 small brown onion (80g), sliced thinly
2 cloves garlic, crushed
2 cups (400g) arborio rice
1 litre (4 cups) chicken stock
½ cup (125ml) dry white wine
700g seafood marinara mix
1 tablespoon finely grated lemon rind
¼ cup (60ml) lemon juice
¼ cup coarsely chopped fresh dill
¼ cup coarsely chopped fresh flat-leaf parsley
4 green onions, sliced thinly

1 Place half of the butter, onion and garlic in large microwave-safe bowl;
   cook, uncovered, on HIGH (100%) about 2 minutes or until onion softens.
   Add rice, stir to coat in butter mixture; cook, uncovered, on HIGH (100%)
   1 minute. Stir in stock and wine; cook, uncovered, on HIGH (100%) for
   15 minutes, pausing to stir every 3 minutes.
2 Stir in marinara mix; cook, uncovered, on HIGH (100%) about 7 minutes
   or until seafood has changed in colour and rice is just tender, stirring once
   during cooking. Stir in remaining ingredients and remaining butter just
   before serving.

SERVES 4
per serving 16.7g fat; 2986kJ (713 cal)

char-grilled tuna with chilled soba

PREPARATION TIME **20 MINUTES** COOKING TIME **15 MINUTES**

Wasabi is Japanese horseradish sold in powdered or paste form. Soba are Japanese buckwheat noodles and are great served hot or cold.

4 x 200g tuna steaks
2 tablespoons mirin
1 tablespoon tamarind puree
400g soba
2 tablespoons toasted
    sesame seeds
4 green onions, sliced thinly
    lengthways
¼ cup (60ml) tamari
1 teaspoon wasabi paste
2 teaspoons sesame oil
2 tablespoons lime juice

1 Place fish in medium bowl with combined mirin and tamarind; toss to coat fish in mirin mixture.
2 Meanwhile, cook soba in large saucepan of boiling water, uncovered, until just tender; drain. Rinse under cold water; drain.
3 Cook fish, in batches, on heated oiled grill plate (or grill or barbecue) until browned both sides and cooked as desired.
4 Combine noodles in medium bowl with seeds and all but 1 tablespoon of the onion. Combine tamari, wasabi, oil and juice in screw-top jar; shake well. Drizzle dressing over noodle mixture; toss gently to combine. Divide noodles among serving plates; top with tuna, sprinkle with remaining onion.

SERVES 4
per serving 19.6g fat;
2905kJ (694 cal)

blue-eye fillets with grilled corn salad

PREPARATION TIME **15 MINUTES** COOKING TIME **20 MINUTES**

4 x 200g blue-eye fillets
2 tablespoons soy sauce

GRILLED CORN SALAD
2 corn cobs (500g), silk
  and husks removed
250g cherry tomatoes, halved
1 small red onion (100g),
  sliced thinly
1 fresh small red thai chilli,
  seeded, sliced thinly
2 medium avocados (500g),
  chopped coarsely
¼ cup coarsely chopped
  fresh coriander
⅓ cup (80ml) lime juice
1 clove garlic, crushed
1 tablespoon olive oil

1 Make grilled corn salad.
2 Brush fish with sauce; cook on
  heated lightly oiled grill plate
  (or grill or barbecue) until
  browned both sides and cooked
  as desired. Serve fish with salad.
  GRILLED CORN SALAD Cook
  corn on heated oiled grill plate
  (or grill or barbecue) until
  browned and just tender;
  cool 10 minutes. Using sharp
  knife, remove kernels from
  cob; combine in medium bowl
  with remaining ingredients.

SERVES 4
per serving 30.2g fat;
2255kJ (539 cal)

prawn green curry

PREPARATION TIME **15 MINUTES** COOKING TIME **15 MINUTES**

1kg uncooked medium king prawns
2 cups (400g) jasmine rice
1 tablespoon peanut oil
1 small brown onion (80g), sliced thinly
1 teaspoon grated fresh ginger
2 kaffir lime leaves, sliced thinly
¼ cup (75g) green curry paste
1⅔ cups (410ml) coconut milk
½ cup (125ml) water
1 tablespoon fish sauce
1 tablespoon lime juice
1 tablespoon brown sugar
100g snake beans, cut into 4cm lengths
¼ cup firmly packed fresh thai basil leaves

1 Shell and devein prawns, leaving tails intact.
2 Cook rice in large saucepan of boiling water, uncovered,
  until just tender; drain. Cover to keep warm.
3 Meanwhile, heat oil in wok or large frying pan; cook onion, ginger,
  lime leaves and paste, stirring, until onion softens. Stir in coconut milk
  and the water; bring to a boil. Reduce heat; simmer, uncovered, 5 minutes.
4 Add prawns to wok with sauce, juice, sugar and beans; simmer, stirring,
  about 5 minutes or until prawns are changed in colour and just cooked
  through. Remove from heat; stir in basil. Serve curry with rice.

SERVES 4
per serving 32.5g fat; 3328kJ (795 cal)

TIP Substitute red curry paste for green curry paste if you prefer.

niçoise salad

PREPARATION TIME **15 MINUTES** COOKING TIME **10 MINUTES**

The original French salade niçoise was created with the finest ingredients grown in Provence – ripe vine tomatoes, local capers, hand-picked baby beans and fresh tuna caught just off the coast. Our version – no less delicious – has adapted a modern approach more suitable to our hectic lifestyle.

200g baby green beans, trimmed
3 medium tomatoes (570g), cut into wedges
4 hard-boiled eggs, quartered
425g can tuna in springwater, drained, flaked
½ cup (80g) drained caperberries, rinsed
½ cup (60g) seeded small black olives
¼ cup firmly packed fresh flat-leaf parsley
440g can whole baby potatoes, rinsed, drained, halved
2 tablespoons olive oil
1 tablespoon lemon juice
2 tablespoons white wine vinegar

1 Boil, steam or microwave beans until just tender; drain. Rinse under cold water; drain.
2 Meanwhile, combine tomato, egg, tuna, caperberries, olives, parsley and potato in large bowl.
3 Combine remaining ingredients in screw-top jar; shake well. Add beans to salad, drizzle with dressing; toss gently to combine.

SERVES 4
per serving 17.8g fat; 1493kJ (357 cal)

TIP This recipe is best made just before serving.

lamb chops with spicy chickpea salad

PREPARATION TIME **15 MINUTES** COOKING TIME **10 MINUTES**

Sumac is an astringent, purple-red spice ground from berries found on shrubs native to the Mediterranean coast. It adds a piquant, tart taste to salads and dips, and is great sprinkled over grilling meats. It is available in most health food stores or Middle-Eastern grocery stores.

8 lamb chump chops (880g)
2 tablespoons olive oil
1 tablespoon finely chopped fresh coriander
2 green onions, chopped finely
2 teaspoons sumac
2 x 400g cans chickpeas, rinsed, drained
4 green onions, sliced thinly
1 small red capsicum (150g), chopped finely
1 large tomato (250g), seeded, chopped finely
1 cup loosely packed fresh coriander leaves

SUMAC DRESSING
¼ cup (60ml) olive oil
2 tablespoons lemon juice
2 tablespoons sweet chilli sauce
2 teaspoons sumac

1 Place lamb in large bowl with combined oil, chopped coriander, chopped onion and sumac; toss to coat lamb in coriander mixture. Cook lamb, in batches, on heated oiled grill plate (or grill or barbecue) until browned both sides and cooked as desired.
2 Meanwhile, make sumac dressing.
3 Combine chickpeas, sliced onion, capsicum, tomato and coriander leaves in large bowl. Add half of the dressing; toss gently to combine. Serve lamb on chickpea salad, drizzled with remaining dressing.
SUMAC DRESSING Combine ingredients in screw-top jar; shake well.

SERVES 4
per serving 52.9g fat; 2942kJ (703 cal)

rosemary and garlic lamb cutlets

PREPARATION TIME **20 MINUTES** COOKING TIME **20 MINUTES**

¼ cup fresh rosemary sprigs
12 lamb cutlets (900g)
3 cloves garlic, crushed
¼ cup coarsely grated lemon rind
2 fresh small red thai chillies,
   seeded, chopped finely
¼ cup (60ml) olive oil
2 cups (500ml) water
1 cup (250ml) chicken stock
¾ cup (120g) polenta
⅓ cup (80ml) milk
½ cup (40g) finely grated
   parmesan cheese
50g butter, melted
2 tablespoons lemon juice

1 Coarsely chop half of the rosemary. Place lamb and chopped rosemary in large bowl with garlic, half of the rind, chilli and oil; toss to coat lamb in rosemary mixture. Cook lamb on heated oiled grill plate (or grill or barbecue) until browned both sides and cooked as desired.

2 Meanwhile, combine the water and stock in large saucepan; bring to a boil. Stir in polenta gradually; cook, stirring, about 10 minutes or until mixture thickens. Add milk and cheese; stir until cheese melts.

3 Divide polenta among serving plates; top with lamb. Drizzle with combined butter and juice, then sprinkle with remaining rind and rosemary.

SERVES 4
per serving 48.1g fat;
2696kJ (644 cal)

pork tikka

PREPARATION TIME **10 MINUTES**
COOKING TIME **20 MINUTES**

2 tablespoons olive oil
1kg pork strips
1 large brown onion (200g),
  sliced thinly
2 cloves garlic, crushed
1 large red capsicum (350g),
  sliced thinly
⅓ cup (100g) tikka masala paste
1 cup (250ml) coconut milk
1 cup (250ml) chicken stock
2 cups (400g) basmati rice
100g snow peas, trimmed
½ cup coarsely chopped
  fresh coriander

1 Heat half of the oil in large
  saucepan; cook pork, in batches,
  until browned.
2 Heat remaining oil in same pan;
  cook onion, garlic and capsicum,
  stirring, until onion softens.
  Return pork to pan with paste;
  cook, stirring, until mixture is
  fragrant. Stir in milk and stock;
  bring to a boil. Reduce heat;
  simmer, uncovered, about
  10 minutes or until sauce
  thickens slightly.
3 Meanwhile, cook rice in large
  saucepan of boiling water,
  uncovered, until just tender;
  drain. Cover to keep warm.
4 Add snow peas and coriander
  to pork; cook, stirring, until
  snow peas are just tender.
  Serve pork tikka with rice.

SERVES 4
per serving 35.3g fat;
4004kJ (957 cal)

asian mini lamb roasts

PREPARATION TIME 15 MINUTES (PLUS STANDING TIME) COOKING TIME 30 MINUTES

Gai larn is also commonly known as gai lum or chinese broccoli;
it is available in most supermarkets and greengrocers.

2 lamb mini roasts (700g)
2 tablespoons kecap manis
1 tablespoon sesame seeds
2 cloves garlic, crushed
2 teaspoons sesame oil
1 teaspoon grated fresh ginger
1 small red capsicum (150g),
   sliced thinly
600g gai larn, chopped coarsely
⅓ cup (80ml) oyster sauce
2 tablespoons water
1 tablespoon lime juice

1 Preheat oven to moderately hot.
2 Cook lamb, uncovered, in heated
   lightly oiled wok or large frying
   pan about 5 minutes or until
   browned. Place lamb on oiled
   wire rack in baking dish; brush
   with combined kecap manis,
   sesame seeds and half of the
   garlic. Roast lamb, uncovered,
   in moderately hot oven about
   25 minutes or until cooked as
   desired. Cover; stand 5 minutes,
   slice thickly.
3 Meanwhile, heat oil in same wok
   or frying pan; stir-fry ginger and
   remaining garlic until fragrant.
   Add remaining ingredients;
   stir-fry until gai larn is just wilted.
   Serve lamb on gai larn mixture,
   drizzled with sauce from wok.

SERVES 4
per serving 22g fat;
1521kJ (363 cal)

chorizo and kumara frittata

PREPARATION TIME **15 MINUTES** COOKING TIME **30 MINUTES**

500g kumara, peeled,
   sliced thinly
¼ cup coarsely chopped
   fresh basil leaves
8 eggs, beaten lightly
½ cup (125ml) milk
1 tablespoon olive oil
1 large brown onion (200g),
   sliced thinly
2 chorizo sausages (340g),
   sliced thinly
120g mesclun
¼ cup (60ml) bottled
   french dressing

1 Preheat oven to hot.
2 Boil, steam or microwave
   kumara until just tender; drain.
3 Meanwhile, combine basil,
   egg and milk in large bowl.
   Heat oil in medium frying pan;
   cook onion and chorizo,
   stirring, until onion softens
   and chorizo is browned.
   Drain on absorbent paper.
4 Add kumara and chorizo mixture
   to egg mixture; pour into oiled
   deep 23cm-square cake pan.
   Bake, uncovered, in hot oven
   about 20 minutes or until frittata
   is just set. Serve frittata with
   combined mesclun and dressing.

SERVES 4
per serving 36.2g fat;
2320kJ (554 cal)

stir-fried lamb in black bean sauce

PREPARATION TIME **15 MINUTES** COOKING TIME **15 MINUTES**

600g lamb strips
1 teaspoon five-spice powder
2 teaspoons sesame oil
2 tablespoons peanut oil
2 cloves garlic, crushed
1 teaspoon grated fresh ginger
1 medium brown onion (150g), sliced thinly
1 small red capsicum (150g), sliced thinly
1 small yellow capsicum (150g), sliced thinly
6 green onions, sliced thinly
1 teaspoon cornflour
½ cup (125ml) chicken stock
1 tablespoon soy sauce
2 tablespoons black bean sauce

1 Place lamb in medium bowl with combined five-spice and
  sesame oil; toss lamb to coat in five-spice mixture.
2 Heat half of the peanut oil in wok or large frying pan; stir-fry lamb,
  in batches, until browned lightly.
3 Heat remaining peanut oil in same wok; stir-fry garlic, ginger
  and brown onion until onion just softens. Add capsicums and
  green onion; stir-fry until capsicum is just tender.
4 Blend cornflour with stock and sauces in small jug. Add cornflour
  mixture to wok with lamb; stir until sauce boils and thickens slightly
  and lamb is cooked as desired.

SERVES 4
per serving 17.4g fat; 1383kJ (331 cal)

beef stroganoff with fettuccine

PREPARATION TIME **15 MINUTES** COOKING TIME **20 MINUTES**

2 tablespoons vegetable oil
600g beef rump steak,
  sliced thinly
1 medium brown onion (150g),
  sliced thinly
2 cloves garlic, crushed
1 teaspoon sweet paprika
400g swiss brown mushrooms,
  sliced thickly
375g fettuccine
2 tablespoons dry red wine
1 tablespoon lemon juice
2 tablespoons tomato paste
1¼ cups (300g) sour cream
1 tablespoon coarsely chopped
  fresh dill

1 Heat half of the oil in large
  frying pan; cook beef, in batches,
  until browned lightly .
2 Heat remaining oil in same pan;
  cook onion and garlic, stirring,
  until onion softens. Add paprika
  and mushrooms; cook, stirring,
  until mushrooms are just tender.
3 Meanwhile, cook pasta in large
  saucepan of boiling water,
  uncovered, until just tender.
4 Return beef to pan with wine
  and juice; bring to a boil. Reduce
  heat; simmer, covered, about
  5 minutes or until beef is tender.
  Add paste, sour cream and
  dill; cook, stirring, until heated
  through. Serve stroganoff
  over drained pasta.

SERVES 4
per serving 50.4g fat;
3991kJ (954 cal)

cajun lamb backstraps with four-bean salad

PREPARATION TIME **15 MINUTES** COOKING TIME **10 MINUTES**

1 tablespoon cajun seasoning
800g lamb backstraps
1 small red onion (100g),
    chopped finely
2 small egg tomatoes (260g),
    chopped coarsely
60g baby spinach leaves,
    shredded finely
2 x 300g cans four-bean mix,
    rinsed, drained
¼ cup firmly packed fresh
    coriander leaves
¼ cup firmly packed fresh
    flat-leaf parsley
⅓ cup (80ml) bottled
    french dressing

1 Using hands, rub seasoning
   onto lamb; cook lamb on
   heated oiled grill plate (or grill
   or barbecue) until browned and
   cooked as desired. Cover; stand
   5 minutes, slice thickly.
2 Meanwhile, place remaining
   ingredients in large bowl; toss
   gently to combine. Serve salad
   topped with lamb.

SERVES 4
per serving 12.5g fat;
1649kJ (394 cal)

veal parmigiana

PREPARATION TIME **15 MINUTES** COOKING TIME **20 MINUTES**

¼ cup (35g) plain flour
2 eggs, beaten lightly
2 tablespoons milk
½ cup (80g) corn flake crumbs
½ cup (50g) packaged breadcrumbs
4 veal schnitzels (360g)
¼ cup (60ml) olive oil
1 medium brown onion (150g), chopped finely
2 cloves garlic, crushed
½ cup (125ml) dry red wine
1½ cups (390g) bottled tomato pasta sauce
1 cup (100g) pizza cheese
200g green beans, trimmed
500g asparagus, trimmed

1 Combine flour, egg and milk in medium bowl; combine corn flake crumbs and breadcrumbs in another medium bowl. Coat veal, one piece at a time, first in egg mixture then in breadcrumb mixture.
2 Heat 2 tablespoons of the oil in large frying pan; cook veal until browned lightly both sides. Place in lightly greased baking dish.
3 Preheat oven to moderately hot.
4 Heat remaining oil in same cleaned pan; cook onion and garlic, stirring, until onion softens. Add wine; bring to a boil. Boil, stirring, 1 minute. Stir in sauce; bring to a boil. Reduce heat; simmer, uncovered, about 5 minutes or until sauce thickens slightly. Cool 5 minutes.
5 Spoon sauce over each piece of veal; top with cheese. Cook, uncovered, in moderately hot oven about 15 minutes or until cheese melts and veal parmigiana is heated through.
6 Meanwhile, boil, steam or microwave beans and asparagus, separately, until just tender; drain. Serve with parmigiana.

SERVES 4
per serving 26g fat; 2512kJ (600 cal)

lamb cutlets with roasted potatoes and tomatoes

PREPARATION TIME **10 MINUTES** COOKING TIME **25 MINUTES**

500g tiny new
  potatoes, quartered
2 tablespoons olive oil
250g grape tomatoes
12 lamb cutlets (900g)
½ cup loosely packed fresh
  basil leaves
½ cup loosely packed fresh
  flat-leaf parsley
1 tablespoon balsamic vinegar

1 Preheat oven to hot.
2 Toss potato and oil in large
   baking dish; roast, uncovered,
   in hot oven 15 minutes. Add
   tomatoes; roast, uncovered,
   about 10 minutes or until
   potato is tender.
3 Meanwhile, cook lamb on
   heated oiled grill plate (or grill
   or barbecue) until browned both
   sides and cooked as desired.
4 Place potato mixture and
   remaining ingredients in medium
   bowl; toss gently to combine.
   Serve lamb on potato mixture.

SERVES 4
per serving 28.9g fat;
1818kJ (434 cal)

roast beef and rocket salad

PREPARATION TIME **10 MINUTES** COOKING TIME **20 MINUTES**

1 tablespoon olive oil
600g piece beef eye fillet
500g tiny new potatoes, halved
120g semi-dried tomatoes
100g baby rocket leaves
1 small red onion (100g),
   sliced thinly
4 green onions, sliced thinly
½ cup (125ml) buttermilk
⅓ cup (100g) mayonnaise
1 tablespoon dijon mustard
1 clove garlic, crushed
1 teaspoon freshly ground
   black pepper

1 Preheat oven to moderately hot.
2 Heat oil in medium flameproof
  baking dish; cook beef, turning,
  until browned. Roast, uncovered,
  in moderately hot oven about
  15 minutes or until cooked as
  desired. Remove from oven.
  Cover; stand 5 minutes, slice
  beef thinly.
3 Meanwhile, boil, steam or
  microwave potato until just
  tender; drain.
4 Combine beef and potato in
  large bowl with tomato, rocket
  and onions. Combine remaining
  ingredients in screw-top jar;
  shake well. Drizzle dressing over
  salad; toss gently to combine.

SERVES 4
per serving 20.9g fat;
2095kJ (501 cal)

TIP Beef can be cooked up to
2 hours ahead; cover, refrigerate
until required.

merguez and couscous salad

PREPARATION TIME **15 MINUTES** COOKING TIME **10 MINUTES**

A small, spicy sausage – believed to have originated in Tunisia but eaten throughout North Africa and Spain – merguez is traditionally made with lamb meat and is easily identified by its chilli-red colour. Merguez can be fried, grilled or roasted, and is most often eaten with couscous; it can be found in many butchers, delicatessens and sausage specialty stores.

500g merguez sausages
1½ cups (375ml) beef stock
1½ cups (300g) couscous
20g butter
1 tablespoon finely grated lemon rind
¾ cup coarsely chopped fresh flat-leaf parsley
120g baby rocket leaves
⅓ cup (50g) toasted pine nuts
2 fresh small red thai chillies, seeded, sliced thinly
1 small red onion (100g), sliced thinly
1 clove garlic, crushed
⅓ cup (80ml) lemon juice
2 tablespoons olive oil

1 Cook sausages on heated grill plate (or grill or barbecue) until browned and cooked through. Drain on absorbent paper; slice thickly.
2 Meanwhile, bring stock to a boil in medium saucepan. Remove from heat; stir in couscous and butter. Cover; stand about 10 minutes or until liquid is absorbed, fluffing couscous with fork occasionally.
3 Place sausage and couscous in large bowl with remaining ingredients; toss gently to combine.

SERVES 4
per serving 45g fat; 3621kJ (865 cal)

lamb and parsley salad kebabs

PREPARATION TIME **25 MINUTES**   COOKING TIME **10 MINUTES**

Sumac is an astringent, purple-red spice ground from berries found on shrubs native to the Mediterranean coast. It adds a piquant, tart taste to salads and dips, and is great sprinkled over grilling meats. It is available in most health food stores or Middle-Eastern grocery stores.

500g lamb fillets
1 tablespoon sumac
1½ cups coarsely chopped fresh flat-leaf parsley
300g can chickpeas, rinsed, drained
1 large tomato (250g), seeded, sliced thinly
1 small red onion (100g), sliced thinly
2 tablespoons lemon juice
1 tablespoon olive oil
250g prepared hummus
4 large pitta
½ cup (60g) coarsely grated cheddar cheese

1 Place lamb and sumac in medium bowl; toss to coat lamb in sumac. Cook lamb on heated oiled grill plate (or grill or barbecue) until browned and cooked as desired. Cover; stand 5 minutes, slice lamb thickly.

2 Meanwhile, combine parsley, chickpeas, tomato, onion, juice and oil in medium bowl.

3 Spread hummus evenly over one side of each pitta. Divide cheese, parsley salad and lamb among pitta; roll to enclose filling, cut kebabs in half to serve.

SERVES 4
per serving 27.7g fat; 2780kJ (664 cal)

beef and mushroom pie

PREPARATION TIME **10 MINUTES** COOKING TIME **20 MINUTES**

2 sheets ready-rolled puff pastry
1 tablespoon olive oil
1 medium brown onion (150g),
 sliced thinly
1 clove garlic, crushed
250g mushrooms, quartered
500g beef rump steak, sliced thinly
1 tablespoon plain flour
½ cup (125ml) dry red wine
½ cup (125ml) beef stock
425g can crushed tomatoes
2 tablespoons tomato paste
2 teaspoons fresh thyme leaves

1 Preheat oven to moderately hot.
2 Cut each pastry sheet into four squares; using sharp knife, score one side of four squares in crosshatch pattern. Place all eight squares on oiled oven trays; bake in moderately hot oven about 15 minutes or until browned lightly.
3 Meanwhile, heat oil in frying pan; cook onion and garlic, stirring, until onion softens. Add mushrooms; cook, stirring, 2 minutes.
4 Toss beef with flour in medium bowl, add to pan; cook, stirring, about 5 minutes or until beef is browned. Stir in wine, stock, undrained tomatoes and paste; bring to a boil. Reduce heat; simmer, uncovered, about 10 minutes or until mixture thickens slightly. Stir in thyme.
5 Divide unscored pastry squares among serving plates; carefully cut large hole in top of each. Fill hole with beef mixture; top with remaining pastry squares, scored-side up.

SERVES 4
per serving 18.2g fat; 1610kJ (385 cal)

beef red curry with rice noodles

PREPARATION TIME **15 MINUTES** COOKING TIME **20 MINUTES**

2 tablespoons peanut oil
750g beef rump steak, sliced thinly
1 small brown onion (80g), sliced thinly
1 small red capsicum (150g), sliced thinly
2 cloves garlic, crushed
¼ cup (75g) red curry paste
3 kaffir lime leaves, sliced thinly
1 cup (250ml) coconut milk
½ cup (125ml) water
800g fresh rice noodles
1 tablespoon fish sauce
1 tablespoon lime juice
1 tablespoon brown sugar
230g can sliced bamboo shoots, drained
1 cup loosely packed fresh coriander leaves

1 Heat half of the oil in large saucepan; cook beef, in batches, until browned all over.
2 Heat remaining oil in same pan; cook onion, capsicum, garlic, paste and lime leaves, stirring, until onion softens. Return beef to pan with coconut milk and the water; bring to a boil. Reduce heat; simmer, uncovered, 10 minutes.
3 Meanwhile, place noodles in large heatproof bowl, cover with boiling water, separate with fork; drain.
4 Add sauce, juice, sugar, bamboo shoots and half of the coriander to curry; stir until heated through. Serve curry on noodles, sprinkled with remaining coriander.

SERVES 4
per serving 42.2g fat; 4026kJ (962 cal)

TIP Commercially prepared red curry pastes can vary in strength and flavour. You may need to adjust the amount you use according to your taste.

chicken and pecan pasta

PREPARATION TIME **15 MINUTES** COOKING TIME **15 MINUTES**

Farfalle is a short pasta variously known as bowties or butterflies. You need to purchase a large barbecued chicken, weighing approximately 1kg, for this recipe.

500g farfalle
2 tablespoons warm water
½ cup (120g) sour cream
½ cup (150g) mayonnaise
1 tablespoon dijon mustard
3 cups (480g) shredded cooked chicken
2 trimmed celery sticks (150g), sliced thinly
1 cup (115g) toasted pecans, halved lengthways
1 small red onion (100g), sliced thinly

1 Cook pasta in large saucepan of boiling water, uncovered, until just tender; drain. Rinse under cold water; drain.
2 Combine the water, sour cream, mayonnaise and mustard in large bowl. Add pasta and remaining ingredients to bowl; toss gently to combine.

SERVES 4
per serving 56.4g fat; 4622kJ (1104 cal)

chinese barbecued pork and rice noodle stir-fry

PREPARATION TIME **15 MINUTES** COOKING TIME **10 MINUTES**

Chinese barbecued pork is
available from Asian grocery
stores and barbecued meat shops.

375g dried rice noodles
1 tablespoon sesame oil
1 clove garlic, crushed
1 fresh small red thai chilli,
  seeded, sliced thinly
350g mushrooms, sliced thickly
2 teaspoons cornflour
¼ cup (60ml) soy sauce
600g chinese barbecued pork,
  sliced thickly
1 tablespoon fish sauce
¾ cup (180ml) chicken stock
8 green onions, sliced thinly

1 Place noodles in large heatproof
  bowl, cover with boiling water,
  stand until just tender; drain.
2 Meanwhile, heat oil in wok or
  large frying pan; stir-fry garlic,
  chilli and mushrooms until
  mushrooms are just tender.
3 Blend cornflour with soy sauce in
  small jug. Add cornflour mixture
  to wok with pork, sauce and
  stock; stir until sauce boils and
  thickens slightly. Add noodles
  and onion; stir-fry until hot.

SERVES 4
per serving 29.1g fat;
2990kJ (714 cal)

spirals with crisp salami and tomato sauce

PREPARATION TIME **15 MINUTES** COOKING TIME **15 MINUTES**

A short pasta, fusilli is shaped like a spiral or corkscrew; very small
spirals are called fusillini. You can use any short pasta you like for this
recipe. Danish salami is a smoked, delicately spiced salami; again,
you can use another variety if you wish.

500g fusilli
1 tablespoon olive oil
200g thinly sliced danish salami
2 cloves garlic, crushed
3 small zucchini (280g), sliced thinly
1 teaspoon dried chilli flakes
700g bottled tomato pasta sauce
1¼ cups (150g) seeded green olives
1 cup coarsely chopped fresh flat-leaf parsley

1 Cook pasta in large saucepan of boiling water, uncovered,
 until just tender.
2 Meanwhile, heat half of the oil in medium frying pan; cook salami,
 stirring, until crisp. Drain on absorbent paper; cut slices into strips.
3 Heat remaining oil in same cleaned pan; cook garlic and zucchini,
 stirring, about 2 minutes or until zucchini is just tender. Stir in salami
 with chilli, sauce and olives; cook, stirring, until heated through.
4 Place drained pasta and zucchini mixture in large bowl with parsley;
 toss gently to combine.

SERVES 4
per serving 28g fat; 3455kJ (825 cal)

asparagus and salmon pasta

PREPARATION TIME **15 MINUTES** COOKING TIME **10 MINUTES**

Shell pasta, or conchiglie, is available in three sizes: in addition to the medium shell we used here, there is a smaller shell called conchigliette, which makes a great addition to soups, and a larger shell, called conchiglioni, which is usually served stuffed and baked.

375g shell pasta
400g asparagus, trimmed
415g can red salmon,
    drained, flaked
100g watercress, trimmed
1 small white onion (80g),
    sliced thinly
1 clove garlic, crushed
2 tablespoons wholegrain
    mustard
2 tablespoons red wine vinegar
2 tablespoons lemon juice
¼ cup (60ml) olive oil

1 Cook pasta in large saucepan of boiling water, uncovered, until just tender; drain. Rinse under cold water; drain.

2 Meanwhile, cut asparagus into 5cm lengths. Boil, steam or microwave asparagus until just tender; drain. Rinse under cold water; drain.

3 Combine pasta and asparagus in large bowl with salmon, watercress and onion. Place remaining ingredients in screw-top jar; shake well. Drizzle dressing over pasta; toss gently to combine.

SERVES 4
per serving 25.2g fat;
2672kJ (638 cal)

grilled lamb and risoni with mustard sauce

PREPARATION TIME **10 MINUTES**
COOKING TIME **25 MINUTES**

Risoni is a small rice-shaped pasta that can be served similarly to orzo or rice in salads and soups.

450g lamb fillets
500g risoni
1 tablespoon olive oil
2 cloves garlic, crushed
300ml cream
¼ cup (70g) wholegrain
  mustard
1 cup (125g) frozen peas

1 Cook lamb, in batches, on heated oiled grill plate (or grill or barbecue) until browned and cooked as desired. Cover; stand 5 minutes, slice thickly.
2 Meanwhile, cook pasta in large saucepan of boiling water, uncovered, until just tender.
3 Heat oil in small saucepan; cook garlic, stirring, until browned lightly. Add cream and mustard; bring to a boil. Reduce heat; simmer, uncovered, 2 minutes. Add peas; bring to a boil then remove from heat.
4 Place drained pasta, lamb and sauce in large bowl; toss gently to combine.

SERVES 4
per serving 44.1g fat;
3934kJ (940 cal)

baked pasta with ham, blue cheese and fennel

PREPARATION TIME **15 MINUTES**   COOKING TIME **30 MINUTES**

375g shell pasta
250g ham, sliced thinly
4 eggs, beaten lightly
300ml cream
½ cup (125ml) milk
200g soft blue-vein
  cheese, crumbled
2 small fennel (400g), trimmed,
  sliced thinly
4 medium egg tomatoes (300g),
  chopped coarsely
1 tablespoon olive oil
¼ cup coarsely chopped
  fresh fennel tips

1 Preheat oven to moderately hot.
2 Cook pasta in large saucepan
  of boiling water, uncovered,
  until just tender.
3 Meanwhile, cook ham in small
  heated frying pan until browned.
4 Combine ham and drained pasta
  in large bowl with egg, cream,
  milk, cheese and fennel. Transfer
  mixture to deep oiled 2-litre
  (8 cup) ovenproof dish. Toss
  tomato in oil in small bowl;
  sprinkle over pasta mixture.
5 Bake, uncovered, in moderately
  hot oven about 15 minutes or
  until heated through. Sprinkle
  with fennel tips before serving.

SERVES 4
per serving 60.7g fat;
4238kJ (1012 cal)

chinese barbecued duck salad

PREPARATION TIME **30 MINUTES** COOKING TIME **5 MINUTES**

Chinese barbecued duck is available from Asian grocery stores
and specialty barbecued meat shops.

1 chinese barbecued duck
200g dried rice stick noodles
¾ cup loosely packed fresh coriander leaves
¾ cup loosely packed fresh mint leaves
2 lebanese cucumbers (260g), seeded, sliced thinly
½ cup (75g) toasted cashews

CHILLI LIME DRESSING
2 fresh large green chillies, seeded, chopped finely
1 stalk fresh lemon grass, chopped finely
1 clove garlic, crushed
1 teaspoon coarsely grated lime rind
¼ cup (60ml) lime juice
2 tablespoons peanut oil
1 tablespoon brown sugar
1 tablespoon fish sauce
2 teaspoons sesame oil

1 Discard skin and bones from duck; chop duck meat coarsely.
2 Place noodles in medium heatproof bowl, cover with boiling water,
stand until just tender; drain. Rinse under cold water; drain.
3 Make chilli lime dressing.
4 Combine duck and noodles in large bowl with herbs and
cucumber, drizzle with dressing; toss gently to combine.
Top with nuts before serving.
CHILLI LIME DRESSING Combine ingredients in screw-top jar; shake well.

SERVES 4
per serving 35g fat; 2712kJ (648 cal)

hot-smoked salmon salad

PREPARATION TIME 15 MINUTES COOKING TIME **15 MINUTES**

While most of the smoked salmon we buy has been cold-smoked (cured at a low temperature for a fairly long time), hot-smoked salmon (cured at high temperatures for just a few hours) is generally moister and not as salty; it doesn't, however, have the same keeping properties as does cold-smoked.

400g hot-smoked salmon
100g mizuna
1 medium avocado (250g),
   chopped coarsely
1 lebanese cucumber (130g),
   halved, sliced thinly
1 small fennel (200g), trimmed,
   sliced thinly
¼ cup (50g) drained baby
   capers, rinsed
375g fettuccine
1 tablespoon dijon mustard
2 teaspoons sugar
2 tablespoons olive oil
1 tablespoon lemon juice

1 Remove any skin and bones from salmon; flake salmon into large pieces. Combine salmon in large bowl with mizuna, avocado, cucumber, fennel and capers.

2 Meanwhile, cook pasta in large saucepan of boiling water, uncovered, until just tender.

3 Combine remaining ingredients in screw-top jar; shake well. Add drained pasta and dressing to salmon mixture; toss gently to combine.

SERVES 4
per serving 25.2g fat;
2769kJ (662 cal)

spaghetti, spinach and fetta frittata

PREPARATION TIME **20 MINUTES**   COOKING TIME **25 MINUTES**

100g spaghetti
150g baby spinach leaves
6 eggs
¼ cup (60ml) vegetable stock
½ cup (125ml) cream
200g fetta cheese, crumbled
2 tablespoons olive oil
1 medium red onion (170g),
   sliced thinly
1 clove garlic, crushed
200g grape tomatoes
250g yellow teardrop tomatoes
1 tablespoon balsamic vinegar

1 Cook pasta in large saucepan of boiling water, uncovered, until just tender; drain. Combine pasta and spinach in large bowl; toss gently until spinach wilts.

2 Meanwhile, whisk eggs in large jug with stock and cream; stir in cheese.

3 Heat half of the oil in deep 24cm heavy-based ovenproof frying pan; cook onion and garlic, stirring, until onion softens. Add pasta mixture then pour in egg mixture, cover; cook over medium heat until frittata is almost set. Uncover; cook under heated grill until frittata is browned lightly and just set.

4 Meanwhile, heat remaining oil in medium frying pan; cook tomatoes until just tender. Remove from heat, add vinegar; toss gently to combine. Serve tomatoes with frittata.

SERVES 4
per serving 41.8g fat;
2383kJ (569 cal)

TIP Cherry tomatoes can be used if grape tomatoes are unavailable.

sukiyaki stir-fry with udon

PREPARATION TIME **20 MINUTES** COOKING TIME **15 MINUTES**

This recipe is a simplified variation of the traditional Japanese cook-at-the-table classic. You need about half a small chinese cabbage to make this recipe. Sukiyaki sauce is a commercially made product consisting mainly of soy sauce and mirin.

350g fresh udon
1 tablespoon peanut oil
500g beef rump steak, sliced thinly
1 large carrot (180g), halved lengthways, sliced thinly
2 trimmed celery sticks (150g), sliced thickly
190g can sliced bamboo shoots, drained
5 green onions, sliced thinly
150g shiitake mushrooms, sliced thinly
300g firm tofu, cut into 2cm cubes
2 cups (160g) coarsely shredded chinese cabbage
¾ cup (180ml) bottled sukiyaki sauce
2 teaspoons brown sugar

1 Place udon in large heatproof bowl, cover with boiling water, separate udon with fork; drain.
2 Heat half of the oil in wok or large frying pan; stir-fry beef, in batches, until browned and cooked as desired.
3 Heat remaining oil in same wok; stir-fry carrot, celery and bamboo shoots until carrot is just tender. Add onion and mushrooms; stir-fry until mushrooms are just tender.
4 Return beef to wok with udon, tofu, cabbage, sauce and sugar; stir-fry until cabbage just wilts.

SERVES 4
per serving 23.6g fat; 3038kJ (726 cal)

peppered swordfish with chilli and chermoulla noodles

PREPARATION TIME **15 MINUTES** COOKING TIME **15 MINUTES**

Chermoulla is a simple, spicy Moroccan sauce or marinade traditionally made of ground spices, including cumin and paprika, and fresh herbs.

2 tablespoons olive oil
1 tablespoon finely grated lemon rind
1 teaspoon cracked black pepper
4 x 200g swordfish steaks
375g dried rice stick noodles
2 fresh small red thai chillies, seeded, chopped finely
2 green onions, chopped finely

CHERMOULLA
⅓ cup (80ml) olive oil
⅓ cup (80ml) lemon juice
½ cup coarsely chopped fresh coriander
2 cloves garlic, crushed
2 teaspoons ground cumin
½ teaspoon hot paprika

1 Combine oil, rind and pepper in large bowl. Add fish; toss gently to coat fish in pepper mixture. Cover; stand 10 minutes.
2 Meanwhile, make chermoulla.
3 Cook fish, in batches, on heated oiled grill plate (or grill or barbecue) until browned and cooked as desired.
4 Meanwhile, place noodles in large heatproof bowl, cover with boiling water, stand until just tender; drain. Return noodles to same dried bowl with chilli, onion and half of the chermoulla; toss gently to combine.
5 Divide noodles among serving plates; top with fish and remaining chermoulla.
CHERMOULLA Combine ingredients in screw-top jar; shake well.

SERVES 4
per serving 33.8g fat; 3102kJ (741 cal)

marinated vegetable pasta

PREPARATION TIME **10 MINUTES** COOKING TIME **15 MINUTES**

Rigatoni is a ridged pasta that looks like thick, short penne; its grooves and wide centre help contain chunky sauces.

2 cloves garlic, crushed
290g jar mixed antipasto, drained, chopped coarsely
340g jar marinated artichokes, drained, quartered
⅓ cup (80ml) vegetable stock
⅓ cup (80ml) dry red wine
700g bottled tomato pasta sauce
500g rigatoni
½ cup coarsely chopped fresh basil
50g parmesan cheese, shaved

1 Cook garlic, antipasto and artichoke in large frying pan, stirring, 3 minutes. Stir in stock, wine and sauce; bring to a boil. Reduce heat; simmer, uncovered, about 5 minutes or until sauce thickens slightly.
2 Meanwhile, cook pasta in large saucepan of boiling water, uncovered, until just tender.
3 Add drained pasta and basil to sauce; toss gently to combine. Divide pasta among serving bowls; top with cheese.

SERVES 4
per serving 10.9g fat; 3022kJ (722 cal)

antipasto puff pastry tartlets

PREPARATION TIME **20 MINUTES** COOKING TIME **20 MINUTES**

¼ cup (60ml) olive oil
2 cloves garlic, crushed
1 small red capsicum (150g), chopped coarsely
1 small yellow capsicum (150g), chopped coarsely
1 medium zucchini (120g), sliced thinly
2 baby eggplants (120g), sliced thinly
1 small red onion (100g), sliced thickly
100g semi-dried tomatoes
150g baby bocconcini cheese, halved
½ cup (40g) finely grated parmesan cheese
½ cup firmly packed fresh basil leaves
2 sheets ready-rolled puff pastry
⅓ cup (85g) bottled tomato pasta sauce
2 tablespoons bottled olive tapenade

1 Preheat oven to moderately hot.
2 Combine oil and garlic in large bowl. Add capsicums, zucchini, eggplant
   and onion; toss gently to coat vegetables in mixture.
3 Cook vegetables, in batches, on heated oiled grill plate (or grill or barbecue)
   until browned lightly and just tender; transfer to large bowl. Add tomatoes,
   cheeses and basil; toss gently to combine.
4 Cut pastry sheets in half; fold edges 1cm inward, place on oiled oven
   trays. Divide sauce among pastry pieces; top with vegetable mixture.
   Bake, uncovered, in moderately hot oven about 15 minutes or until
   browned lightly. Serve tartlets topped with tapenade.

SERVES 4
per serving 29.8g fat; 1794kJ (429 cal)

dhal with minted cucumber yogurt

PREPARATION TIME **20 MINUTES** COOKING TIME **25 MINUTES**

Garam masala, a blend of spices favoured by cooks in North India,
is based on varying proportions of cardamom, cinnamon, cloves,
coriander, fennel and cumin, roasted and ground together.
Black pepper and chilli can be added for a spicier version.

1 litre (4 cups) water
2 cups (400g) red lentils
1 teaspoon ground turmeric
2 teaspoons cumin seeds
2 teaspoons black mustard seeds
2 tablespoons ghee
4 green onions, sliced thinly
2 fresh small red thai chillies, chopped finely
2 tablespoons grated fresh ginger
2 cloves garlic, crushed
1 small tomato (130g), seeded, chopped finely
2 teaspoons garam masala
12 pappadums

MINTED CUCUMBER YOGURT
2 lebanese cucumbers (260g), seeded, chopped finely
1 cup (280g) yogurt
½ cup loosely packed fresh mint leaves, sliced thinly
¼ cup (60ml) lime juice

1 Combine the water, lentils and turmeric in large saucepan; bring
to a boil. Reduce heat; simmer, uncovered, about 15 minutes or
until lentils are tender, stirring occasionally.
2 Meanwhile, make minted cucumber yogurt.
3 Cook seeds in large heated frying pan, stirring until fragrant.
Add ghee, onion, chilli, ginger, garlic and tomato; cook, stirring,
5 minutes. Add lentil mixture to pan; stir over low heat until
heated through. Remove from heat; stir in garam masala.
4 Meanwhile, place 3 pappadums around edge of microwave
oven turntable. Cook on HIGH (100%) about 30 seconds or
until puffed; repeat with remaining pappadums. Serve dhal
with pappadums and minted cucumber yogurt.
MINTED CUCUMBER YOGURT Combine ingredients in small bowl.

SERVES 4
per serving 13.7g fat; 1923kJ (459 cal)

lentil and caramelised onion soup

PREPARATION TIME **10 MINUTES** COOKING TIME **25 MINUTES**

2 cups (400g) red lentils
½ cup (100g) brown rice
1 litre (4 cups) vegetable stock
1 litre (4 cups) water
1 tablespoon ground cumin
40g butter
3 medium brown onions (450g),
   sliced thinly
2 tablespoons sugar
1 tablespoon balsamic vinegar
pinch cayenne pepper
⅓ cup coarsely chopped
   fresh coriander
⅓ cup coarsely chopped fresh
   flat-leaf parsley
1 cup (250ml) vegetable
   stock, extra

1 Rinse lentils and rice under
cold water; drain.
2 Combine stock and the water
in large saucepan; bring to a boil.
Add lentils, rice and cumin; return
to a boil. Reduce heat; simmer,
uncovered, stirring occasionally,
about 15 minutes or until lentils
and rice are just tender.
3 Meanwhile, melt butter in large
frying pan; cook onion, stirring,
until onion softens. Add sugar
and vinegar; cook, stirring,
until onion caramelises.
4 Stir pepper, coriander and parsley
into lentil mixture; bring to a boil.
Stir in caramelised onion and
extra stock; cook, stirring,
until heated through.

SERVES 4
per serving 12.2g fat;
2125kJ (508 cal)

vegetable, haloumi and rocket salad

PREPARATION TIME **15 MINUTES**
COOKING TIME **15 MINUTES**

250g haloumi cheese,
    cut into 2cm cubes
180g mushrooms, halved
1 medium red capsicum (200g),
    chopped coarsely
1 medium yellow capsicum
    (200g), chopped coarsely
3 baby eggplants (180g),
    chopped coarsely
2 medium zucchini (320g),
    sliced thickly
2 tablespoons olive oil
2 tablespoons balsamic vinegar
1 clove garlic, crushed
150g baby rocket leaves

1 Cook cheese, mushrooms,
  capsicums, eggplant and
  zucchini, in batches, on heated
  oiled grill plate (or grill or
  barbecue) until browned
  lightly and just tender.
2 Meanwhile, place oil, vinegar
  and garlic in screw-top jar;
  shake well.
3 Combine cheese and vegetables
  in large bowl with rocket and
  dressing; toss gently to combine.

SERVES 4
per serving 20.7g fat;
1229kJ (294 cal)

avocado caesar salad

PREPARATION TIME **20 MINUTES** COOKING TIME **5 MINUTES**

2 small white bread rolls (80g), sliced thinly
1 clove garlic, crushed
1 tablespoon olive oil
2 baby cos lettuce, torn
1 large red onion (300g), sliced thinly
2 medium avocados (500g), chopped coarsely
⅓ cup (50g) sun-dried tomatoes in oil, drained, sliced thinly
60g parmesan cheese, shaved

DRESSING
1 clove garlic, crushed
2 egg yolks
2 teaspoons dijon mustard
2 tablespoons white vinegar
1 cup (250ml) extra light olive oil

1 Preheat oven to moderately hot.
2 Place bread slices, in single layer, on oven tray; brush with combined garlic and oil. Toast in moderately hot oven about 5 minutes or until crisp.
3 Meanwhile, make dressing.
4 Combine toast in large bowl with remaining ingredients and dressing; toss gently to combine.
DRESSING Blend or process garlic, yolks, mustard and vinegar until smooth. With motor operating, gradually add oil in a thin steady stream; process until mixture thickens.

SERVES 4
per serving 90.5g fat; 3942kJ (942 cal)

TIP Garlic toasts can be made a day ahead; store in an airtight container.

italian-style stuffed mushrooms

PREPARATION TIME 15 MINUTES COOKING TIME **15 MINUTES**

Marsala is a sweet fortified wine originally from Sicily; it can be found in liquor stores.

8 medium flat
   mushrooms (800g)
90g butter
½ medium red capsicum (100g),
   chopped finely
1 clove garlic, crushed
¼ cup (60ml) marsala
1 tablespoon lemon juice
1½ cups (110g) stale
   breadcrumbs
2 tablespoons coarsely chopped
   fresh flat-leaf parsley
1 cup (80g) coarsely grated
   pecorino cheese

1 Preheat oven to moderately hot.
2 Carefully remove stems from
   mushrooms; chop stems finely.
3 Melt butter in small frying pan.
   Brush mushroom caps with
   about half of the butter; place
   on oiled oven trays.
4 Cook capsicum and garlic,
   stirring, in remaining butter
   until capsicum is just tender.
   Add chopped stems, marsala,
   juice and breadcrumbs; cook,
   stirring, 3 minutes. Remove from
   heat; stir in parsley and cheese.
   Spoon filling into mushroom caps;
   bake, uncovered, in moderately
   hot oven about 10 minutes
   or until browned lightly.

SERVES 4
per serving 25.6g fat;
1868kJ (446 cal)

TIP Vegetable stock can be
substituted for marsala, if desired.

spinach and leek risotto

PREPARATION TIME **10 MINUTES** COOKING TIME **40 MINUTES**

½ cup (125ml) dry white wine
1 litre (4 cups) vegetable stock
2 cups (500ml) water
80g butter
1 medium leek (350g),
  sliced thinly
2 cloves garlic, crushed
2 cups (400g) arborio rice
180g baby spinach leaves
½ teaspoon ground nutmeg
1 cup (80g) finely grated
  parmesan cheese

1 Combine wine, stock and the
  water in medium saucepan;
  bring to a boil. Reduce heat;
  simmer, covered.
2 Meanwhile, melt 60g of the
  butter in large saucepan; cook
  leek and garlic, stirring, until leek
  softens. Add rice; stir to coat in
  leek mixture. Stir in 1 cup of
  the simmering stock mixture;
  cook, stirring, over low heat
  until liquid is absorbed. Continue
  adding simmering stock mixture,
  in 1-cup batches, stirring, until
  liquid is absorbed after each
  addition. Total cooking time
  should be about 35 minutes
  or until rice is tender. Gently
  stir in spinach, nutmeg, cheese
  and remaining butter.

SERVES 4
per serving 24.8g fat;
2744kJ (656 cal)

TIP Risotto should be creamy;
if it's too thick, you can add
a little boiling water.

gnocchi with spinach cream sauce

PREPARATION TIME **10 MINUTES** COOKING TIME **15 MINUTES**

600g fresh gnocchi
30g butter
1 medium brown onion (150g), chopped finely
1 clove garlic, crushed
½ cup (125ml) dry white wine
¾ cup (180ml) cream
¾ cup (180ml) vegetable stock
300g baby spinach leaves, shredded coarsely
½ cup (40g) finely grated parmesan cheese

1 Cook gnocchi in large saucepan of boiling water, uncovered, about 5 minutes or until gnocchi float to the surface; drain.
2 Meanwhile, melt butter in large saucepan; cook onion and garlic, stirring, until onion softens. Stir in wine, cream and stock; bring to a boil. Boil, uncovered, 2 minutes.
3 Add spinach and cheese; cook, stirring, until spinach is just wilted and cheese melts. Serve gnocchi topped with spinach cream sauce.

SERVES 4
per serving 27.8g fat; 2158kJ (515 cal)

eggplant, spinach and pumpkin stacks

PREPARATION TIME **15 MINUTES** COOKING TIME **15 MINUTES**

1 large eggplant (500g)
coarse cooking salt
200g pumpkin, sliced thinly
700g bottled tomato pasta sauce
80g baby spinach leaves
4 green onions, sliced thinly lengthways
1 cup (100g) coarsely grated
  mozzarella cheese
¼ cup (40g) toasted pine nuts

1 Discard top and bottom of eggplant; cut eggplant lengthways into ten 5mm slices. Discard rounded-skin-side slices; place remaining eight slices in colander, sprinkle all over with salt; stand 10 minutes.

2 Rinse eggplant well under cold water; pat dry with absorbent paper. Cook eggplant and pumpkin, in batches, on heated oiled grill plate (or grill or barbecue) until tender.

3 Meanwhile, place sauce in medium saucepan; bring to a boil. Reduce heat; simmer, uncovered, 2 minutes.

4 Place four slices of the eggplant, in single layer, on oven tray; top with half of the spinach, half of the pumpkin and half of the onion. Spoon 2 tablespoons of the sauce over each then repeat layering process, using remaining spinach, pumpkin, onion and another 2 tablespoons of the sauce for each stack. Top stacks with remaining eggplant slices; pour over remaining sauce, sprinkle stacks with cheese and nuts. Place under hot grill until cheese browns lightly.

SERVES 4
per serving 14.4g fat; 1143kJ (275 cal)

TIP Weight the eggplant when draining to extract as much water as possible; otherwise, the liquid causes the eggplant to soften and lose its shape when cooked. This process is called degorging.

cauliflower and broccoli curry

PREPARATION TIME **20 MINUTES** COOKING TIME **15 MINUTES**

1 tablespoon peanut oil
2 tablespoons red curry paste
1 large red capsicum (350g),
   sliced thinly
1 tablespoon honey
3⅓ cups (830ml) coconut cream
1 cup (250ml) water
500g broccoli, chopped coarsely
500g cauliflower,
   chopped coarsely
425g can whole baby corn
   spears, drained
500g choy sum,
   chopped coarsely

1 Heat oil in large saucepan; cook
paste, stirring, until fragrant.
Add capsicum; cook, stirring,
until almost tender.
2 Stir in honey, coconut cream
and the water; bring to a boil.
Add broccoli and cauliflower,
reduce heat; simmer, uncovered,
2 minutes. Add corn and choy
sum; cook, stirring, until choy
sum just wilts.

SERVES 4
per serving 51g fat;
2657kJ (635 cal)

TIP Different brands of
commercially prepared curry
pastes vary in strength and
flavour, so you may want to
adjust the amount of paste
to suit your taste.

panzanella

PREPARATION TIME **15 MINUTES** COOKING TIME **10 MINUTES**

This Italian bread salad was originally created as a way of using up stale bread – but our version, made with fresh wood-fired ciabatta, is even more delicious. Many varieties of cooked white beans are available canned, among them cannellini, butter and haricot beans; any of these is suitable for this salad.

½ long loaf ciabatta (250g)
1 clove garlic, crushed
¼ cup (60ml) olive oil
500g cherry tomatoes, halved
1 lebanese cucumber (130g), seeded, sliced thinly
1 medium avocado (250g), chopped coarsely
¼ cup (50g) drained capers, rinsed
1 large yellow capsicum (350g), chopped coarsely
2 x 400g cans white beans, rinsed, drained
½ cup coarsely chopped fresh basil

TOMATO VINAIGRETTE
½ cup (125ml) tomato juice
¼ cup (60ml) red wine vinegar
⅓ cup (80ml) olive oil

1 Preheat oven to moderately hot.
2 Cut bread into 2cm cubes. Combine bread in large bowl with combined garlic and oil; toss to coat bread in oil mixture. Place bread, in single layer, on oven tray; bake in moderately hot oven about 10 minutes or until browned lightly.
3 Meanwhile, make tomato vinaigrette.
4 Place bread in same large bowl with remaining ingredients and vinaigrette; toss gently to combine.
TOMATO VINAIGRETTE Combine ingredients in screw-top jar; shake well.

SERVES 4
per serving 45.8g fat; 2556kJ (611 cal)

TIP Ciabatta is readily available from most supermarkets; however, any crisp-crusted Italian bread can be used in this recipe.

tofu and sugar snap pea stir-fry

PREPARATION TIME **25 MINUTES (PLUS STANDING TIME)** COOKING TIME **15 MINUTES**

Mirin is a sweetened rice wine used in Japanese cooking; it is sometimes referred to in cookbooks simply as rice wine. You can substitute sweet white wine, or even sherry, if mirin is unavailable.

600g firm tofu
1 tablespoon sesame oil
1 large red onion (300g),
    sliced thickly
2 cloves garlic, crushed
2 teaspoons grated fresh ginger
1 teaspoon cornflour
⅓ cup (80ml) soy sauce
400g sugar snap peas, trimmed
1 tablespoon brown sugar
⅓ cup (80ml) oyster sauce
2 tablespoons mirin
¼ cup coarsely chopped
    fresh coriander

1 Preheat oven to moderately hot.
2 Weight tofu between two boards; stand, tilted, 10 minutes. Cut tofu into 2cm cubes; pat tofu dry between layers of absorbent paper. Place tofu on baking-paper-lined oven trays. Bake, uncovered, in moderately hot oven about 10 minutes or until browned lightly.
3 Heat oil in wok or large frying pan; stir-fry onion, garlic and ginger until onion softens. Add blended cornflour and soy sauce to wok with tofu, peas, sugar, oyster sauce and mirin; stir-fry until sauce boils and thickens slightly. Remove from heat; stir in chopped coriander.

SERVES 4
per serving 15.4g fat;
1289kJ (308 cal)

herb frittata with mushroom sauce

PREPARATION TIME **15 MINUTES** COOKING TIME **15 MINUTES**

1 tablespoon olive oil
400g button mushrooms, halved
500g swiss brown
    mushrooms, halved
1 clove garlic, crushed
1 tablespoon soy sauce
300ml cream
½ cup (60g) coarsely grated
    cheddar cheese
¾ cup coarsely chopped
    fresh flat-leaf parsley
8 eggs
¾ cup (180ml) cream, extra
1 cup (250ml) vegetable stock
1 tablespoon coarsely chopped
    fresh thyme leaves

1 Heat oil in large deep frying pan;
   cook mushrooms and garlic,
   stirring, about 5 minutes or until
   mushrooms are just tender. Add
   sauce; cook, stirring, 1 minute.
   Stir in cream; bring to a boil.
   Reduce heat; simmer, uncovered,
   about 5 minutes or until sauce
   thickens slightly. Stir in cheese
   and a third of the parsley.
2 Meanwhile, whisk eggs, extra
   cream, stock, thyme and
   remaining parsley in large bowl.
   Pour egg mixture into heated
   oiled 24cm flameproof frying
   pan, cover; cook over medium
   heat about 5 minutes or until
   almost set. Uncover; place under
   hot grill until frittata sets and top
   is browned lightly. Serve frittata
   topped with mushroom sauce.

SERVES 4
per serving 65.3g fat;
3046kJ (728 cal)

vegetable tagine with olive and parsley couscous

PREPARATION TIME **20 MINUTES** COOKING TIME **20 MINUTES**

You need a piece of pumpkin weighing approximately 600g for this recipe.

1 tablespoon olive oil
1 medium red onion (170g), sliced thinly
2 cloves garlic, crushed
1 teaspoon dried chilli flakes
1 teaspoon ground coriander
½ teaspoon ground turmeric
1 teaspoon cumin seeds
500g pumpkin, chopped coarsely
2 medium potatoes (400g), chopped coarsely
2½ cups (625ml) vegetable stock
300g can chickpeas, rinsed, drained
½ cup coarsely chopped fresh coriander

OLIVE AND PARSLEY COUSCOUS
1½ cups (375ml) vegetable stock
1½ cups (300g) couscous
30g butter
1⅓ cups (200g) seeded kalamata olives
½ cup coarsely chopped fresh flat-leaf parsley

1 Heat oil in medium saucepan; cook onion, garlic and chilli, stirring, until onion softens. Add spices and seeds; cook, stirring, until fragrant. Add pumpkin and potato; stir to coat vegetables in spice mixture.
2 Stir in stock; bring to a boil. Reduce heat; simmer, uncovered, about 10 minutes or until vegetables are almost tender. Stir in chickpeas; simmer, uncovered, about 10 minutes or until vegetables in tagine are tender.
3 Meanwhile, make olive and parsley couscous.
4 Stir coriander into tagine. Divide couscous among serving bowls; top with vegetable tagine.
OLIVE AND PARSLEY COUSCOUS Bring stock to a boil in medium saucepan. Remove from heat; stir in couscous and butter. Cover; stand about 5 minutes or until liquid is absorbed, fluffing with fork occasionally. Stir in olives and parsley.

SERVES 4
per serving 14.4g fat; 2541kJ (607 cal)

grilled fruit kebabs with passionfruit sauce

PREPARATION TIME **15 MINUTES**   COOKING TIME **15 MINUTES**

You need about 6 passionfruit for this recipe, as well as 8 skewers. If using bamboo skewers, soak them in water for at least 1 hour before using to avoid them splintering or scorching. We used Cointreau in our sauce, but you can use triple-sec, Grand Marnier or any orange-flavoured liqueur you like; you can also choose to use no alcohol at all.

½ cup (125ml) water
¼ cup (60ml) orange juice
½ cup (110g) caster sugar
1 tablespoon honey
½ cup (125ml) passionfruit pulp
2 tablespoons orange-flavoured liqueur
1 small pineapple (800g), chopped coarsely
1 small pawpaw (650g), chopped coarsely
2 large bananas (460g), sliced thickly
250g strawberries

1 Combine the water, juice, sugar and honey in small saucepan. Stir over heat, without boiling, until sugar dissolves; bring to a boil. Reduce heat; simmer, uncovered, without stirring, about 8 minutes or until mixture thickens slightly. Remove from heat; stir in passionfruit pulp and liqueur. Cool 5 minutes.
2 Thread fruit onto skewers; brush with passionfruit sauce. Cook kebabs on heated oiled grill plate (or grill or barbecue) until browned lightly, brushing occasionally with passionfruit sauce. Serve kebabs drizzled with remaining passionfruit sauce.

SERVES 4
per serving 0.5g fat; 141kJ (338 cal)

coconut rice with mango

PREPARATION TIME **15 MINUTES**

You will need to cook about ¾ cup of medium-grain rice for this recipe.

300ml thickened cream
½ cup (125ml) coconut cream
½ cup (80g) icing sugar mixture
2¼ cups (340g) cooked
  medium-grain white rice
1 large mango (600g),
  chopped coarsely
½ cup (25g) toasted
  flaked coconut

1 Beat cream, coconut cream and sugar in small bowl with electric mixer until soft peaks form.

2 Place rice in large bowl; fold in cream mixture. Cover; refrigerate while preparing mango.

3 Blend or process three-quarters of the mango until smooth; slice remaining mango into thin strips. Divide rice mixture and mango puree, in alternate layers, among four 1-cup (250ml) glasses; top with mango strips and coconut.

SERVES 4
per serving 38.6g fat; 2541kJ (607 cal)

TIP Substitute pawpaw or berries for mango if desired.

minty chocolate mousse

PREPARATION TIME 15 MINUTES (PLUS REFRIGERATION TIME)

150g dark eating
   chocolate, melted
4 eggs, separated
2 tablespoons crème de menthe
1 tablespoon caster sugar

1 Combine chocolate, egg yolks and liqueur in large bowl.

2 Beat egg whites and sugar in small bowl with electric mixer until soft peaks form. Fold into chocolate mixture in two batches.

3 Divide mousse mixture among six ¾-cup (180ml) glasses, cover; refrigerate about 15 minutes or until set. Serve with fresh raspberries if desired.

SERVES 6
per serving 10.7g fat; 905kJ (216 cal)

TIP You can replace the crème de menthe with any liqueur of your choice or, if making for children, use lime cordial (concentrate) instead.

apple and rhubarb turnovers

PREPARATION TIME **15 MINUTES** COOKING TIME **25 MINUTES**

2 medium apples (300g)
20g butter
2 cups (220g) coarsely chopped trimmed rhubarb
⅓ cup (75g) firmly packed brown sugar
1 tablespoon lemon juice
½ teaspoon ground cinnamon
2 sheets ready-rolled butter puff pastry
1 egg, beaten lightly
1 tablespoon icing sugar mixture

1 Preheat oven to moderately hot.
2 Peel and core apples; cut into thin wedges. Melt butter in medium frying pan; cook apple, rhubarb, sugar and juice, stirring occasionally, until sugar dissolves and apple starts to caramelise. Stir in cinnamon; spread mixture on tray. Cool 10 minutes.
3 Cut two 14cm rounds from each pastry sheet. Place a quarter of the fruit mixture on each pastry round; brush around edges with egg. Fold pastry over to enclose filling; pinch edges together to seal. Place turnovers on lightly greased oven tray; brush with egg.
4 Bake, uncovered, in moderately hot oven about 15 minutes or until turnovers are browned lightly. Dust with sifted icing sugar; serve warm with cream or ice-cream, if desired.

SERVES 4
per serving 7.8g fat; 885kJ (211 cal)

mocha trifle

PREPARATION TIME 25 MINUTES

It is important the chocolate is cool, but not set, before it is added to the custard. You can use either Kahlúa or Tia Maria in this recipe.

1 tablespoon boiling water
2 tablespoons instant
  coffee powder
2 tablespoons coffee-
  flavoured liqueur
1 cup (250ml) vanilla custard
100g dark eating
  chocolate, melted
300ml thickened cream
300g plain chocolate cake
300g raspberries

1 Combine the water, coffee and liqueur in small jug; stir until coffee dissolves.
2 Combine custard and chocolate in small bowl; fold in whipped thickened cream.
3 Halve cake horizontally; trim one half to fit base of deep round 2-litre (8 cup) serving bowl; drizzle with half of the coffee mixture. Sprinkle half of the raspberries over coffee mixture then spread with half of the custard mixture. Repeat with remaining cake, coffee mixture, raspberries and custard mixture. Cover; refrigerate 10 minutes.

SERVES 4
per serving 53.7g fat; 3488kJ (833 cal)

pancakes with choc-hazelnut sauce

PREPARATION TIME **15 MINUTES**   COOKING TIME **20 MINUTES**

1 cup (150g) self-raising flour
1 tablespoon caster sugar
1 cup (250ml) milk
1 teaspoon vanilla essence
1 egg
20g butter, melted
200ml vanilla ice-cream

CHOC-HAZELNUT SAUCE
150g dark eating chocolate,
   chopped coarsely
⅔ cup (160ml) cream
¼ cup (90g) golden syrup
2 tablespoons hazelnut-
   flavoured liqueur
20g butter

1 Combine flour and sugar in
   medium bowl; make well in
   centre. Gradually whisk in
   combined milk, essence, egg
   and butter; strain batter into
   large jug.
2 Cook ¼ cups of the batter,
   in batches, in large heated
   oiled non-stick frying pan until
   browned lightly both sides.
3 Make choc-hazelnut sauce.
4 Top pancakes with ice-cream;
   drizzle with choc-hazelnut sauce.
   CHOC-HAZELNUT SAUCE
   Combine ingredients in small
   saucepan; stir over heat,
   without boiling, until smooth.

SERVES 4
per serving 43.5g fat;
3385kJ (809 cal)

berry sponge slice

PREPARATION TIME **15 MINUTES** COOKING TIME **25 MINUTES**

Use the frozen berries unthawed to minimise their colour "bleeding" into the sponge mixture. Fresh mixed berries can also be used instead of frozen.

2 sheets ready-rolled sweet puff pastry
3 eggs
½ cup (110g) caster sugar
½ cup (75g) self-raising flour
1 cup (150g) frozen mixed berries
1 egg white, beaten lightly
1 tablespoon caster sugar, extra

BERRY COMPOTE
¼ cup (60ml) water
¼ cup (55g) caster sugar
1 teaspoon finely grated lemon rind
1 cup (150g) frozen mixed berries

1 Preheat oven to hot. Grease 25cm x 30cm swiss roll pan. Roll one pastry sheet large enough to cover base of prepared pan.
2 Beat eggs and sugar in small bowl with electric mixer until thick and creamy; fold in sifted flour. Spread mixture evenly over pastry in pan; sprinkle with berries.
3 Roll remaining pastry sheet large enough to fit pan; carefully place over berries. Brush pastry with egg white, sprinkle with extra sugar; carefully score pastry in crosshatch pattern. Bake, uncovered, in hot oven about 20 minutes or until pastry is browned lightly and crisp.
4 Meanwhile, make berry compote.
5 Serve slice with berry compote and cream, if desired.
   BERRY COMPOTE Combine the water and sugar in small saucepan; stir over heat, without boiling, until sugar dissolves. Add rind and berries; stir until hot.

SERVES 8
per serving 15.6g fat; 1768kJ (423 cal)

steamed jam puddings

PREPARATION TIME 15 MINUTES   COOKING TIME 25 MINUTES

Serve these puddings warm with vanilla custard or cream.

⅓ cup (110g) raspberry jam
1 egg
½ cup (110g) caster sugar
1 cup (150g) self-raising flour
½ cup (125ml) milk
25g butter, melted
1 tablespoon boiling water
1 teaspoon vanilla essence

1 Preheat oven to moderate. Grease four ¾-cup (180ml) metal moulds; divide jam among moulds.
2 Beat egg and sugar in small bowl with electric mixer until thick and creamy. Fold in sifted flour and milk, in two batches, then combined butter, water and essence.
3 Top jam with pudding mixture. Place moulds in medium baking dish; pour enough boiling water into dish to come halfway up sides of moulds. Bake, uncovered, in moderate oven about 25 minutes. Stand 5 minutes; turn onto serving plates.

SERVES 4
per serving 8.1g fat; 1624kJ (388 cal)

TIP You can use any flavour of jam for this recipe.

mini lime cheesecakes

**PREPARATION TIME 15 MINUTES
(PLUS REFRIGERATION TIME)**

200g plain sweet biscuits
125g butter, melted
250g cream cheese, softened
¾ cup (165g) caster sugar
1 tablespoon finely grated
   lime rind
2 tablespoons lime juice
300ml thickened cream

1 Grease four 11cm-round
   loose-based flan tins.
2 Blend or process biscuits
   until mixture resembles fine
   breadcrumbs. Add butter;
   process until just combined.
   Press biscuit mixture evenly
   over bases and around sides of
   prepared tins, cover; refrigerate
   while preparing filling.
3 Beat cheese, sugar, rind and
   juice in small bowl with electric
   mixer until smooth.
4 Beat cream in small bowl with
   electric mixer until soft peaks
   form; fold into cheese mixture.
   Spoon filling into prepared tins,
   cover; refrigerate 15 minutes.

SERVES 4
per serving 82g fat;
4535kJ (1083 cal)

TIP You can substitute lemon rind
and juice for the lime, if desired.

orange almond cakes with cardamom syrup

PREPARATION TIME **15 MINUTES (PLUS STANDING TIME)** COOKING TIME **20 MINUTES**

80g butter, softened
2 teaspoons finely grated orange rind
½ cup (110g) caster sugar
3 eggs
1½ cups (185g) almond meal
⅓ cup (50g) rice flour
⅓ cup (25g) flaked almonds, chopped finely

CARDAMOM SYRUP
1 medium orange (240g)
½ cup (110g) caster sugar
½ cup (125ml) water
6 cardamom pods, bruised

1 Preheat oven to moderate. Grease six ½-cup (125ml) oval
or rectangular friand pans; place on oven tray.
2 Beat butter, rind and sugar in small bowl with electric mixer
until light and fluffy. Beat in eggs, one at a time, beating
until combined between additions. Mixture may curdle at this
stage but will come together later. Stir in almond meal, flour
and almonds. Divide mixture among prepared pans; bake,
uncovered, in moderate oven about 20 minutes.
3 Meanwhile, make cardamom syrup.
4 Stand cakes 5 minutes then turn onto wire rack over tray;
turn top-side-up, pour hot syrup over hot cakes.
CARDAMOM SYRUP Using vegetable peeler, remove rind
from orange; shred rind finely. Juice the orange; place
⅓ cup (80ml) of juice in small saucepan with shredded rind,
sugar, the water and cardamom. Stir over heat, without
boiling, until sugar dissolves; bring to a boil. Boil, uncovered,
without stirring, about 10 minutes or until mixture
thickens slightly; discard cardamom, transfer syrup
to small heatproof jug.

SERVES 6
per serving 33g fat; 2183kJ (521 cal)

butterscotch and white chocolate fondue

PREPARATION TIME 10 MINUTES (PLUS STANDING TIME) COOKING TIME **10 MINUTES**

Serve this fondue with the fresh fruit of your choice. We particularly like banana, kiwi fruit, pear, apple and strawberries.

1 cup (200g) firmly packed
    brown sugar
⅓ cup (115g) golden syrup
50g butter
300ml cream
100g white eating chocolate,
    chopped coarsely

1 Combine sugar, golden syrup, butter and cream in medium saucepan, stir over heat until sugar dissolves and butter melts; bring to a boil. Boil, uncovered, 1 minute. Remove from heat; cool 5 minutes.
2 Add chocolate; stir until smooth. Stand 10 minutes before serving.

SERVES 6
per serving 30.7g fat;
2096kJ (501 cal)

TIP The cream mixture must be cooled for 5 minutes before adding chocolate to avoid the chocolate "seizing", that is, becoming grainy and firm and having the appearance of a dull paste.

ice-cream with choc-peanut sauce

PREPARATION TIME 5 MINUTES (PLUS STANDING TIME) COOKING TIME **10 MINUTES**

You can use either Kahlúa or
Tia Maria in this recipe.

2 x 60g Snickers chocolate bars,
   chopped coarsely
½ cup (125ml) cream
2 tablespoons coffee-
   flavoured liqueur
1 litre (4 cups) vanilla ice-cream

1 Place Snickers and cream in
   small saucepan; cook, stirring,
   without boiling, until Snickers
   melt and sauce thickens slightly.
   Remove from heat.
2 Stir in liqueur; stand 5 minutes
   before serving drizzled over
   scoops of ice-cream.

SERVES 4
per serving 48.7g fat;
3152kJ (753 cal)

glossary

almond

MEAL also known as ground almonds; nuts are powdered to a coarse flour-like texture, for use in baking or as a thickening agent.

bamboo shoots tender young shoots of a particular variety of bamboo, available fresh or canned.

beans

GREEN sometimes called french or string beans, this thin fresh bean is consumed pod and all.

SNAKE long (about 40cm), thin, round, fresh green beans; Asian in origin, with a taste similar to green or french beans. Used most frequently in stir-fries, they are also called yard-long beans because of their length.

black bean sauce a Chinese sauce made from fermented soy beans, spices, water and wheat flour; used in stir-fries.

bok choy also called pak choi or chinese white cabbage; has a fresh, mild mustard taste and is good braised or in stir-fries. Baby bok choy is also available and is slightly more tender than bok choy.

butter use salted or unsalted ("sweet") butter; 125g is equal to one stick of butter.

buttermilk originally the liquid left after cream was separated from milk, today it is commercially made similarly to yogurt.

cajun seasoning used to give an authentic American Deep South spicy cajun flavour to food, this blend of assorted herbs and spices can include paprika, basil, onion, fennel, thyme, cayenne and tarragon.

caperberries fruit formed after the caper buds have flowered; caperberries are pickled, usually with stalks intact, and are used whole.

capers the grey-green buds of a warm climate (usually Mediterranean) shrub, sold either dried and salted or pickled in a vinegar brine.

capsicum also known as bell pepper or, simply, pepper. Native to Central and South America, they can be red, green, yellow, orange or purplish-black. Discard seeds and membranes before use.

cayenne pepper a thin-fleshed, long, extremely hot dried red chilli, usually purchased ground; both arbol and guajillo chillies are the fresh sources for cayenne.

cheese

BLUE mould-treated cheeses mottled with blue veining. Varieties include firm and crumbly stilton types to mild, creamy brie-like cheeses.

BOCCONCINI walnut-sized, fresh, baby mozzarella; a delicate, semi-soft, white cheese traditionally made in Italy from buffalo milk. Spoils rapidly so must be kept under refrigeration, in brine, for one or two days at most.

HALOUMI a firm, cream-coloured sheep-milk cheese matured in brine; somewhat like a minty, salty fetta in flavour, haloumi can be grilled or fried, briefly, without breaking down.

PECORINO a hard, white to pale-yellow cheese, traditionally made from sheep milk; varieties are named after the region in which the cheese is produced – romano from Rome, sardo from Sardinia, siciliano from Sicily, and so forth.

chilli available in many different types and sizes, both fresh and dried. Generally the smaller the chilli, the hotter it is. Use rubber gloves when seeding and chopping fresh chillies as they can burn your skin.

FLAKES crushed dried chillies.

THAI RED small, medium-hot chillies that are bright-red in colour.

chorizo sausage a sausage of Spanish origin, made of coarsely ground pork and highly seasoned with garlic and chillies.

choy sum also known as pakaukeo or flowering cabbage; a member of the bok choy family that is easily identified with its long stems, light green leaves and yellow flowers. Eaten, stems and all, either steamed or stir-fried.

cointreau a French liqueur; orange-flavoured brandy that is 40% alcohol by volume.

coriander also known as cilantro or chinese parsley when fresh; bright-green leafy herb with a pungent flavour often stirred into a dish just before serving for maximum impact. Also sold dried, as seeds or ground.

cornflour also known as cornstarch; used as a thickening agent in cooking.

cos lettuce also known as romaine lettuce, this is the traditional Caesar-salad lettuce. This long-leafed, tightly furled salad green is thought to have originated on the Aegean island of Cos.

couscous fine, grain-like cereal product, originally from North Africa; made from semolina.

crème de menthe crisp, fresh-tasting peppermint-flavoured liqueur.

cucumber

LEBANESE short, slender and thin-skinned; this variety is also known as the european or burpless cucumber.

TELEGRAPH long and green in colour with thin ridges running down its entire length; it is also known as continental cucumber.

egg some recipes in this book call for raw or barely cooked eggs; exercise caution if there is a salmonella problem in your area.

eggplant purple-skinned vegetable also known as aubergine. Can be bought char-grilled in jars.

fish sauce also known as nam pla or nuoc nam; made from pulverised, salted, fermented fish, most often anchovies. Has a pungent smell and strong taste; use sparingly. There are many kinds, of varying intensity.

five-spice powder a fragrant blend of ground cinnamon, clove, star anise, sichuan pepper and fennel.

flour

PLAIN an all-purpose flour, made from wheat.

RICE a very fine flour, made from ground white rice.

SELF-RAISING plain flour sifted with baking powder in the proportion of 1 cup flour to 2 teaspoons baking powder.

ghee clarified butter; once the milk solids are removed, the remaining fat can be heated to high temperatures without burning or smoking.

golden syrup a by-product of refined sugarcane; pure maple syrup or honey can be substituted.

hummus Middle-Eastern salad or dip made from chickpeas, garlic, lemon juice and tahini (sesame seed paste); buy ready-made from supermarkets and delicatessens.

ice-cream we used a good quality ice-cream having 5g of fat per 100ml.

kaffir lime leaves also known as bai magrood, sold fresh, dried or frozen. From the kaffir lime tree, the fruit of which is also used in cooking. Dried leaves are far less potent than fresh so double the amount if you use them.

kecap manis also known as ketjap manis; an Indonesian thick soy sauce which has had sugar and spices added.

kumara Polynesian name of orange-fleshed sweet potato often confused with yam.

lemon grass a tall, clumping, lemon-smelling and -tasting, sharp-edged grass; the white lower part of each stem is chopped and used in Asian cooking and to make tea.

lemon pepper seasoning a blend of crushed black pepper, lemon, herbs and spices.

lime pickle an Indian condiment made of lime, vinegar, peanut oil, salt and spices. It is usually very hot so use sparingly.

lychees hard-skinned fruit with a delicate texture and flavour; to use fresh, peel away the rough skin and remove the seed. They are also available in cans.

mince meat also known as ground meat.

mirin sweet rice wine used in Japanese cooking. Sometimes referred to simply as rice wine but should not be confused with sake, rice wine made for drinking.

mushrooms

FLAT large, flat mushrooms having a rich earthy flavour, ideal for filling and barbecuing. They are sometimes mistakenly called field mushrooms, which grow in the wild rather than being cultivated like flats.

SHIITAKE also sold as donko mushrooms; available fresh and dried. Have a unique meaty flavour, which is stronger when dried.

SWISS BROWN also known as roman or cremini; light- to dark-brown mushrooms with full-bodied flavour. Button or cap mushrooms can be substituted.

oyster sauce Asian in origin; this sauce is made from oysters and their brine, cooked with salt and soy sauce, and thickened with starches.

pappadums sun-dried wafers made from a combination of lentil and rice flours, oil and spices.

parsley, flat-leaf also known as continental parsley or italian parsley.

patty-pan squash also known as crookneck or custard marrow pumpkins; a round, slightly flat summer squash being yellow to pale green in colour and having a scalloped edge. Harvested young, it has firm white flesh and distinct flavour.

pine nuts also known as pignoli; not really nuts but small, cream-coloured kernels from the cones of several types of pine tree.

pitta also known as lebanese bread. This wheat-flour pocket bread is sold in large, flat pieces that separate into two thin rounds. Also available in small thick pieces called pocket pitta.

polenta also known as cornmeal; a flour-like cereal made of dried corn (maize) sold ground in several different textures. Also the name of the dish made from it.

preserved lemon whole or quartered salted lemons preserved in a mixture of olive oil and lemon juice; a North African speciality usually added to casseroles and tagines for their rich salty-sour flavour. Available from good food shops and delicatessens. Rinse well under cold water before using; discard pulp and use finely chopped rind.

rocket also known as arugula, rugula and rucola; a peppery-tasting green leaf which can be used in cooking or eaten raw in salad. Baby rocket leaves are smaller and less peppery.

sambal oelek (also ulek or olek) Indonesian in origin; a salty paste made from ground chillies and vinegar.

snickers a chocolate confectionery made from milk chocolate, peanuts, glucose, sugar, milk powder, butter and egg white.

sugar

BROWN extremely soft, fine granulated sugar containing molasses for its characteristic colour and flavour.

CASTER also known as superfine or finely granulated table sugar.

ICING SUGAR MIXTURE also known as confectioners' sugar or powdered sugar; granulated sugar crushed together with a small amount (about 3%) of cornflour added.

sugar snap peas also known as honey snap peas; fresh small pea which is eaten whole, pod and all, similarly to a snow pea.

tapenade a thick paste made from olives, anchovies, olive oil, lemon, capers and spices.

thai basil also known as horapa; different from holy basil and sweet basil in both look and taste. Having smaller leaves and purplish stems, it is slightly licorice or aniseed tasting, and is one of the basic flavours synonymous with Thai cuisine.

tofu also known as bean curd; an off-white, custard-like product made from the "milk" of crushed soy beans. Available fresh as soft or firm, and processed as fried or pressed dried sheets. Leftover fresh tofu can be refrigerated in water (which is changed daily) up to four days.

tomato

EGG also called plum or roma, these are smallish and oval-shaped.

GRAPE small, grape-shaped tomatoes similar in texture and colour to cherry tomatoes but having a richer, fuller flavour.

PASTA SAUCE prepared sauce available bottled from supermarkets.

SAUCE also known as ketchup or catsup; a condiment made from tomatoes, vinegar and various spices.

SEMI-DRIED partially dried tomato sections, usually sold marinated in a herbed olive oil mixture.

tamari naturally-brewed Japanese soy sauce; made from soy beans, salt, wheat, alcohol and water.

vanilla essence this inexpensive substitute for pure vanilla extract is made with synthetic vanillin and other flavourings. Available from supermarkets.

vinegar

BALSAMIC originally from Modena, Italy, there are now many balsamic vinegars on the market ranging in pungency and quality depending on the method and time they have been aged. Quality can be determined up to a point by price; use the most expensive sparingly.

MALT made from fermented malt and beech shavings.

RED WINE based on fermented red wine.

WHITE WINE made from white wine.

wasabi an Asian horseradish used to make the pungent, green-coloured sauce traditionally served with Japanese raw fish dishes; sold in powdered or paste form.

yogurt we used unflavoured full-fat yogurt in our recipes unless stated otherwise.

zucchini also known as courgette; belonging to the squash family.

index

facts & figures

Wherever you live, you'll be able to use our recipes with the help of these easy-to-follow conversions. While these conversions are approximate only, the difference between an exact and the approximate conversion of various liquid and dry measures is minimal and will not affect your cooking results.

dry measures

metric	imperial
15g	1/2oz
30g	1oz
60g	2oz
90g	3oz
125g	4oz (1/4lb)
155g	5oz
185g	6oz
220g	7oz
250g	8oz (1/2lb)
280g	9oz
315g	10oz
345g	11oz
375g	12oz (3/4lb)
410g	13oz
440g	14oz
470g	15oz
500g	16oz (1lb)
750g	24oz (11/2lb)
1kg	32oz (2lb)

oven temperatures

These oven temperatures are only a guide. Always check the manufacturer's manual.

	°C (Celsius)	°F (Fahrenheit)	Gas Mark
Very slow	120	250	1
Slow	150	300	2
Moderately slow	160	325	3
Moderate	180 - 190	350 - 375	4
Moderately hot	200 - 210	400 - 425	5
Hot	220 - 230	450 - 475	6
Very hot	240 - 250	500 - 525	7

liquid measures

metric	imperial
30ml	1 fluid oz
60ml	2 fluid oz
100ml	3 fluid oz
125ml	4 fluid oz
150ml	5 fluid oz (1/4 pint/1 gill)
190ml	6 fluid oz
250ml	8 fluid oz
300ml	10 fluid oz (1/2 pint)
500ml	16 fluid oz
600ml	20 fluid oz (1 pint)
1000ml (1 litre)	13/4 pints

helpful measures

metric	imperial
3mm	1/8in
6mm	1/4in
1cm	1/2in
2cm	3/4in
2.5cm	1in
5cm	2in
6cm	21/2in
8cm	3in
10cm	4in
13cm	5in
15cm	6in
18cm	7in
20cm	8in
23cm	9in
25cm	10in
28cm	11in
30cm	12in (1ft)

measuring equipment

The difference between one country's measuring cups and another's is, at most, within a 2 or 3 teaspoon variance. (For the record, one Australian metric measuring cup holds approximately 250ml.) The most accurate way of measuring dry ingredients is to weigh them. When measuring liquids, use a clear glass or plastic jug with the metric markings. (One Australian metric tablespoon holds 20ml; one Australian metric teaspoon holds 5ml.)

If you would like to purchase *The Australian Women's Weekly* Test Kitchen's metric measuring cups and spoons (as approved by Standards Australia), turn to page 120 for details and order coupon. You will receive:

- a graduated set of four cups for measuring dry ingredients, with sizes marked on the cups.
- a graduated set of four spoons for measuring dry and liquid ingredients, with amounts marked on the spoons.

Note: North America, NZ and the UK use 15ml tablespoons. All cup and spoon measurements are level.

We use large eggs having an average weight of 60g.

how to measure

When using graduated metric measuring cups, shake dry ingredients loosely into the appropriate cup. Do not tap the cup on a bench or tightly pack the ingredients unless directed to do so. Level top of measuring cups and measuring spoons with a knife. When measuring liquids, place a clear glass or plastic jug with metric markings on a flat surface to check accuracy at eye level.

Looking after **your interest...**

Keep your ACP cookbooks clean, tidy and within easy reach with slipcovers designed to hold up to 12 books. Plus you can follow our recipes perfectly with a set of accurate measuring cups and spoons, as used by *The Australian Women's Weekly* Test Kitchen.

To order

Mail or fax Photocopy and complete the coupon below and post to ACP Books Reader Offer, ACP Publishing, GPO Box 4967, Sydney NSW 2001, or fax to (02) 9267 4967.

Phone Have your credit card details ready, then phone 136 116 (Mon-Fri, 8.00am-6.00pm; Sat, 8.00am-6.00pm).

Price

Book Holder

Australia: $13.10 (incl. GST).
Elsewhere: $A21.95.

Metric Measuring Set

Australia: $6.50 (incl. GST).
New Zealand: $A8.00.
Elsewhere: $A9.95.

Prices include postage and handling.
This offer is available in all countries.

Payment

Australian residents

We accept the credit cards listed on the coupon, money orders and cheques.

Overseas residents

We accept the credit cards listed on the coupon, drafts in $A drawn on an Australian bank, and also British, New Zealand and U.S. cheques in the currency of the country of issue. Credit card charges are at the exchange rate current at the time of payment.

Photocopy and complete coupon below

- -

☐ **Book Holder**

☐ **Metric Measuring Set**
   Please indicate number(s) required.

Mr/Mrs/Ms _____

Address _____

_____

Postcode _____ Country _____

Ph: Business hours (   ) _____

I enclose my cheque/money order for $ _____ payable to ACP Publishing.

OR: please charge my

☐ Bankcard   ☐ Visa   ☐ Mastercard

☐ Diners Club   ☐ American Express

| | | | | | | | | | | | | | | | | | |
Card number

Expiry date ____ /____

Cardholder's signature _____

Please allow up to 30 days delivery within Australia.
Allow up to 6 weeks for overseas deliveries.
Both offers expire 31/12/04. HLMMIM03

Test Kitchen Staff
Food director *Pamela Clark*
Food editor *Karen Hammial*
Assistant food editor *Amira Ibram*
Test kitchen manager *Kimberley Coverdale*
Home economists *Belinda Black,*
Emma Braz, Sammie Coryton,
Kelly Cruickshanks, Cathie Lonnie,
Christina Martignago, Jeanette Seamons,
Jessica Sly, Kate Tait, Alison Webb
Editorial coordinator *Rebecca Steyns*

ACP Books Staff
Editorial director *Susan Tomnay*
Creative director *Hieu Chi Nguyen*
Senior editor *Julie Collard*
Designer *Caryl Wiggins*
Studio manager *Caryl Wiggins*
Editorial coordinator *Caroline Lowry*
Editorial assistant *Karen Lai*
Publishing manager (sales) *Brian Cearnes*
Publishing manager (rights & new projects)
Jane Hazell
Brand manager *Donna Gianniotis*
Pre-press *Harry Palmer*
Production manager *Carol Currie*
Business manager *Sally Lees*
Chief executive officer *John Alexander*
Group publisher *Jill Baker*
Publisher *Sue Wannan*

Produced by ACP Books, Sydney.
Printed by Dai Nippon Printing in Korea.
Published by ACP Publishing Pty Limited,
54 Park Street, Sydney.
GPO Box 4088, Sydney, NSW 1028.
Ph: (02) 9282 8618 Fax: (02) 9267 9438
acpbooks@acp.com.au
www.acpbooks.com.au
To order books, phone 136 116.
Send recipe enquiries to:
recipeenquiries@acp.com.au
AUSTRALIA: Distributed by Network Services,
GPO Box 4088, Sydney, NSW 1028.
Ph: (02) 9282 8777 Fax: (02) 9264 3278
UNITED KINGDOM: Distributed by Australian
Consolidated Press (UK), Moulton Park
Business Centre, Red House Rd,
Moulton Park, Northampton, NN3 6AQ.
Ph: (01604) 497 531 Fax: (01604) 497 533
acpukltd@aol.com
CANADA: Distributed by Whitecap Books Ltd,
351 Lynn Ave, North Vancouver, BC, V7J 2C4.
Ph: (604) 980 9852 Fax: (604) 980 8197
customerservice@whitecap.ca
www.whitecap.ca
NEW ZEALAND: Distributed by Netlink
Distribution Company, ACP Media Centre,
Cnr Fanshawe and Beaumont Streets,
Westhaven, Auckland.
PO Box 47906, Ponsonby, Auckland, NZ.
Ph: (9) 366 9966 ask@ndcnz.co.nz

Clark, Pamela.
Midweek Meals in Minutes.

Includes index.
ISBN 1 86396 306 5

1. Quick and easy cookery. I. Title: Australian
Women's Weekly. (Series: Meals in Minutes)

641.555

© ACP Publishing Pty Limited 2003
ABN 18 053 273 546
This publication is copyright. No part of it
may be reproduced or transmitted in any form
without the written permission of the publishers.

The publishers would like to thank
Orson & Blake, Woollahra, NSW,
for props used in photography.